FIELD OF DREAMS

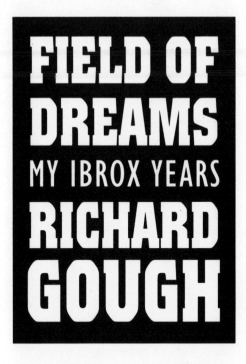

FIELD OF DREAMS
MY IBROX YEARS
RICHARD GOUGH

WITH

KEN GALLACHER

MAINSTREAM
PUBLISHING

EDINBURGH AND LONDON

First published in Great Britain in 1993 by
MAINSTREAM PUBLISHING COMPANY
(EDINBURGH) LTD
7 Albany Street
Edinburgh EH1 3UG
Reprinted 1993

ISBN 1 85158 570 2

A catalogue record for this book is available from the
British Library

Typeset in Palatino by Litho Link Ltd, Welshpool, Powys
Printed in Great Britain by Butler & Tanner Ltd, Frome,
Somerset

Contents

CHAPTER ONE

I'm No Diplomat

Diplomacy has never been one of my strong points and perhaps, at times during my career, that has damaged me. But I won't change and I don't think I should have to change. I see myself as having been an honest person, someone who has not sat on the fence very often and who has expressed strong opinions. I don't see anything wrong with that even though it has brought me into conflict with various people at various times.

There may have been occasions when I could have taken a step back, or *should* have taken a step back, and then said the right thing rather than the honest thing. But I'm afraid I just cannot be like that and I know there are times when I have hurt myself by being honest. Times when my reputation has gone on the line because something I have said has turned out to be controversial when all I have done is state my honest view.

Being as single-minded as I am does bring problems in its wake. I suppose there are times when, as captain of Rangers, I have tried to be as diplomatic as possible. I have never offered outrageous views on anything in the game. But if there is a subject that I have strong feelings

7

about then I speak my mind. It has brought me trouble – but, at the same time, if I had not possessed that strength of will then my career in football might never have taken off at all.

It was my self-belief which carried me through the rejection at Ipswich and the unhappy stay I had at Charlton and allowed me to try again in Scotland . . .

It was my self-belief which sustained me after Rangers gave me that knock-back when I arrived there for the first time on trial. And it was my strength of will which helped me through the tough times I had when I was just a kid trying to make my way over here. I can remember the first time my Mother came to visit me and saw how I was living. She wanted me to return home with her but I wanted to be a professional footballer. She found that hard to understand because she knew what I had left behind me in South Africa. I could have had a comfortable life there – a house with a swimming pool, sunshine instead of the cold and the rain and a home which was light years away from the digs I was staying in. None of that mattered. All I had in my sights was a football career and success in the game and I stuck determinedly to these aims.

Of course the same attitude has brought me into conflict with people in the game . . .

My relationship with Jim McLean died when I stood firm on what I saw as a matter of principle and insisted on being transferred or being paid the kind of money that a valuable asset should have been paid. When Jim would not agree to paying me anything other than what was in my contract I was between a rock and a hard place and I knew it. But I fought for what I believed was right and while I may have lost the relationship with the Dundee United manager I kept faith with myself, and I won – which is maybe why he spoke so badly about me afterwards.

Recently I had a similar clash with the Scotland manager Andy Roxburgh after he had given broad hints to journalists that I was to be axed from the Scotland captaincy and from his squad of players.

When I asked him about these suggestions his answer was that the journalists were simply making mischief. I thought, therefore, that it would be in the interests of both of us if he set the record straight at his next Press Conference. That was due 24 hours after our telephone conversation and Andy Roxburgh, for whatever reason, did not confirm me as his captain and as a member of the squad.

I thought he had been wrong in the first instance to hint that I was finished without discussing that with me. But he was even more wrong when he made no comment after assuring me that I was in his plans, that I was still captain of my country and that the rumours were unfounded. When that happened I knew that I could not play for the man again. It was as simple as that and I made the announcement 48 hours after playing in the Scottish Cup final. I was then criticised for the timing of my statement – but the events had not been precipitated by me. I had consistently refused to discuss the affair with journalists after the team manager's initial remarks. If he had put the matter right then nothing would have been said – he reneged on that statement to me. When that happened any trust or respect in the relationship was gone.

Yet it could all have been avoided. I had spoken to close friends about the international situation and reached the view myself that Andy Roxburgh might begin to phase some of the older players out when it was clear that we had failed to qualify for the World Cup finals in the United States. If he had approached me and talked that through then I would have stayed on as long as I was required to help out while he blooded younger lads. There would have been no problem, no headlines and no controversy.

All the problems came when I felt the manager had let me down. And I still fail to see why I should be criticised for speaking my mind. At least I came straight out and said my piece instead of throwing out hints to sections of the Press.

Anyhow, despite the occasional worries my outspoken nature has given me and the difficulties my strong will has handed me I do believe the positive things which have happened in my life – stemming from the same traits of character – far outweigh them.

I would not change anything at all. People can take me or leave me, but I know what they get from me is honesty and a strong belief in principles. If I say I will do something then I'll do it. All I expect is the same treatment in return. It's when others don't live up to the standards I try to set that I find myself in trouble . . .

And I don't see that coming to an end yet.

CHAPTER TWO

The Troubles with Andy – and the End of My Scotland Career

The relationship between Andy Roxburgh and myself – as Scotland manager and captain – ended last summer. But to be totally blunt it was a relationship which never gelled from the day he first took over as international team boss.

Even during my time as captain I cannot honestly say that the chemistry worked even though I tried very hard to make things work between us. Quite honestly, by that time, I had had too many let-downs, too many problems with the man, to ever be totally comfortable with him. Before Andy was appointed to the post by the SFA in 1986 I had played under two other Scottish managers – the late Jock Stein who was, quite simply, a legend by that stage of his career, and Alex Ferguson, who was in charge part-time as we went to the World Cup finals in Mexico. I had enormous respect for both and I cannot remember any occasion when either of them came even close to calling the number of team meetings Andy insisted upon.

By the time Andy had been in charge for a couple of internationals he had probably had more meetings than Big Jock and Fergie put together. He is not as bad now, but in the beginning whenever training was over – and on some

11

occasions before it started – Andy was calling one meeting after another. As he grew into the job the meetings became fewer. But initially, it reached the stage where Andy seemed to be calling meetings to arrange still more meetings.

Football players are restless people away from training and playing. They get bored easily and even more easily than normal when they have to attend meetings. It became a joke among the players and the training routines which he worked out with his assistant Craig Brown were almost as big a joke! From being a highly professional set-up it became less professional as far as I was concerned. There was not the same air of professionalism that there had been in previous times and all the meetings in the world could not help disguise that fact from the players.

As well as that we began to play teams which were not the strongest teams at our disposal. And that happened – and still happens – because Andy has certain players who *must* play in every match and others are moved around to keep as many players happy as possible. What happened in most cases was that we fielded teams with people playing out of position. It always amazed me to see just how Andy would juggle players around so that he could try to make sure there were no complaints from players who might otherwise be left out. You had Steve Nicol, who was for a long time the finest right-back in Britain, being played at left-back. Or even in midfield. When I was at Spurs and Rangers I was playing centre-back regularly for my club – but I was going in at right-back for my country. After Graeme Souness quit international football Jim Bett was possibly the most effective midfield player in the country – playing in a central role. Andy stuck him out on the flank. Roy Aitken was a superb central defender for Celtic – Andy kept pushing him into midfield where Roy, great motivator and tremendous defender that he was, was never as comfortable. It brought Roy a lot of criticism and yet he was not to blame. He was out of position – or, certainly out of his best position. I felt the same after playing for a spell at the heart of the defence and then being asked to move to full-back.

When I first broke into the team Jock Stein handed me my jersey and told me, 'I've picked you because of what you do for your club – just go out there and do the same tonight.' You could do that because the role was the same as the one you performed at club level. You were familiar with it and comfortable in it. For far too many players Andy Roxburgh could not give them as simple a message because he wanted them to do something they were not doing with their clubs. Jim Bett stopped playing for his country because of that long before my decision to quit Scotland. When John Collins said he was unhappy at playing in a wide midfield role he was left out of the European Championship finals' squad for Sweden. Players simply accepted the problems of having to adapt because they wanted to keep on playing international football – but it was, and it remains, a policy which is wrong for Scotland.

It seems to be fairly well known that some of my own problems began on a long haul flight to Saudi Arabia for a friendly international there 18 months or so after Andy's reign began. But I had had a brush with Craig Brown earlier than that on the bitterly cold night in Belgium. At our training session on the night before we lost 4–1 in Brussels, I was wearing my track suit bottoms when Craig Brown told me to take them off. 'All the players have to look the same,' he told me. I pointed out how cold it was and kept them on. I don't think he ever forgave me.

Then there was the incident on the plane going to the friendly in Saudi and a follow-up in the hotel at the end of the flight. On the flight – much longer than most journeys we have to undertake in Europe – all these games had been organised to kill time and keep the players amused. I think, if I remember correctly, there were card games involved and I just don't play cards. Besides which I just wanted to rest. The games involved teams of three players playing against each other and also had you moving from one row of seats to another until everyone had met. It was like musical chairs thirty thousand feet up and it was not my idea of fun. I was told that I 'had to play'. I told him where to go and I was told I was 'spoiling the game' when I refused to take part. I couldn't believe it but I realised then just why it was that Graeme Souness simply laughed each time Andy Roxburgh's name was mentioned. My Rangers boss at the time didn't take the international manager seriously and I was beginning to understand his attitude!

At the hotel I was in trouble again. Innocently this time. I went downstairs with my room-mate soon after checking in and ordered a snack in the coffee shop. It was just something like hamburger and chips and we were looking around for the rest of the lads. No one was around, which did have me wondering if there had been some mix up.

No meal had been formally arranged and we just assumed that we had to go down to the restaurant and get something. We were wrong. Andy appeared and told us that he had been round the rooms and ordered the players to go to bed. He seemed to take the needle that I was having something to eat without asking his permission. It was a matter of no importance to me and I doubt if it would have offended most other managers but he was angry for some reason or other and I knew then that I was fighting a losing battle with the man.

14

The first major public row came in 1990 during the World Cup finals in Italy when I travelled to Genoa with the squad even though I knew I was suffering from an injury which had been recurring throughout the previous season while I was playing with Rangers. Looking back now it's possible that I should have called off from the finals and then I would not have suffered as I did when I had to fly home.

But, at the time, I wanted to go to Italy. I had played in Mexico four years earlier and having tasted that atmosphere once I wanted to do so again. Also I had been criticised during the run-up to the finals because I had missed Scotland games – and my absences had been down to the same injury which was still troubling me. I had had two operations and I thought the trouble had been cleared up. It had been a problem because we could not find out what was wrong and it was later the doctors discovered it was a Morton's Neuroma – which affects the nerves – between my toes and the sole of my foot. I played against Egypt at Pittodrie and felt it flare up again just before we were to go to Malta for our last preparations. The ground was hard and I think that brought on the recurrence initially. I told Andy Roxburgh and the backroom staff all knew the problem I was having. In Malta I took scarcely any part in training in case I did any further damage but the trouble was monitored on an almost daily basis. Perhaps I should have told Andy to tell the Press that I had a problem . . . but that was really his decision. He saw the Press on a daily basis in Malta and in Italy and he said nothing. That's how I came to be regarded as the villain of the piece when I limped off at half time in the opening game against Costa Rica!

I had told Andy before the match that despite the pain and despite the problem I was having with the injury, I was willing to give it a go if that's what he wanted. He agreed knowing full well the risk involved. But when I broke down it was left looking as if it was my fault. I was more or less accused of letting Scotland down by saying I was fit when I wasn't. If Andy Roxburgh had been open with the Press then the facts would have been known. If he had handled the whole affair the way England boss Bobby Robson handled his captain Bryan Robson's Achilles problem then I would not have faced the homecoming hassle from reporters and photographers at Glasgow Airport.

They were convinced that some story lay behind this supposed 'mysterious' injury. The headlines were about me instead of about the defeat Scotland suffered against the supposed rabbits of the group. In June I saw a specialist in Harley Street – something I should have done almost a year earlier. I had one operation and then, later, I had another to remove a neuroma which had been hidden first time round.

To this day I still cannot understand why I was sneaked out of the hotel in Italy. I expected to be at a Press Conference to explain to everyone what had happened. I wasn't afforded that opportunity because I was whisked away in secret – adding to the supposed 'mystery'. Perhaps that suited Andy but it was in stark contrast to the way his England counterpart chose to handle Bryan Robson's problems. Bryan flew home a hero – I was being pilloried.

At that time I thought long and hard in the summer about playing for Scotland again but my father and Walter Smith both told me that I should continue and I did. Predictably Andy blamed the Press for the whole sorry misunderstanding. That was an excuse I was to hear again before my final decision to quit Scotland was made.

A little more than a year later I was back in the squad for the European Championship game against Switzerland in Berne – and found myself in the centre of an action replay of that World Cup incident.

When I joined the squad I told Andy that I had picked up a thigh knock playing for Rangers but, hopefully, I would be OK for the game in Berne. On the Monday I could not train but Andy asked me to do interviews for television and I told them that I was looking forward to the game and that we hoped for a good result. At that time I still thought I would be ready. Then, on the Tuesday night, after doing a little bit of training – but not too much – I had a rub in my room from Jimmy Steel, the masseur with the side. Now, for me and for almost every player you could speak to, Steely is the best. He has worked with Celtic and with Scotland for many years and has tremendous experience. We would all swear by him.

He felt something there in the thigh. I asked him about the injury and his opinion was that I would not be 100 per cent fit and all I would do if I played was run the risk of causing further damage. In the morning there was still no improvement and I then told Andy that there was a risk if I played in the game. I stressed to him that I did not want a repeat of what had happened against Costa Rica in Genoa and he agreed. He thanked me for being upfront with him, for being honest with him.

Of course, I did not have a hint of what was being said, of what was going on behind the scenes. As far as I was concerned Andy had told me he had brought adequate cover and he had known from the off that there was a doubt – in fact the injury would keep me out of Rangers' next game.

But in the stadium as I sat in the stand a journalist came to ask me how I was and told me that Andy had told the Press that I had been passed fit to play. At first I didn't believe the story. The next day as we flew home more Pressmen approached me to say that Andy was insisting that his 'medical staff' had declared me fit to play. This was nonsense. The doctor, the physios and the masseur had all known of the injury problem I had. When I got to Glasgow Airport I saw it in print – headlines blaring out to the whole country that I had been fit but had not played.

By now my head was reeling and suggestions were surfacing that Andy had said I would not play for Scotland again. I was furious. I could not believe that all of this was happening to me. At the baggage reclaim I was looking for him to get an explanation while some of the players were trying to calm me down. After all these trips Andy has a set routine where he goes round all the players to shake their hands – such a lovely guy, you know – and there he is coming towards me with his hand outstretched. I could not credit it. How could the man want to shake my hand after the stories he had told? I knocked his hand away, just slapped it aside and asked him about the headlines and about what he had said to the Press. As always he started to blame the journalists, saying that words had been taken out of context.

I pointed out that it was difficult to take anything out of context when he was making such strong statements about me – when he was apparently saying things that just were not true. I told him a few home truths then in less than Parliamentary language and I did let him have it because I was convinced that my Scotland career was now over. I could not see me ever playing for him again. I told him straight that this was the second time he had done this to me, the second time he had involved me in controversy through no fault of mine. Normally, I said, managers are there to protect their players not throw them to the wolves. And I told him that the injury was so troublesome that even though Rangers had an important game against Dundee United on the Saturday I would miss it.

To be honest I came very close to hitting him. I thought about it because of the anger I felt at the injustice of it all. But

I wanted to retain some dignity and I am glad now I didn't hit him though I was *awfully* close to doing it.

Walter Smith took up the matter with him and he said the Press had made too much of it and that it was all a storm in a teacup. By now the medical staff had backed me, I had missed the following game and Andy had to backtrack. This time he backtracked so much that he made me his captain not too long after that. I went back – again on Walter's advice – but the wounds were still there. They had never healed properly and although I captained the side in the European Championship finals I knew the relationship would never be 100 per cent right.

We did well enough there, and give Andy Roxburgh credit, one of the reasons for that was the camaraderie which grew in the squad during our ten days' trip to the United States and Canada. The trip was criticised – I suppose because it was partly a holiday trip with just two games thrown in – but the short tour worked. It brought the lads together and that's why we were relatively successful in Sweden. There was a club feeling about the group which went there and that came from the jaunt across the Atlantic.

Although I was captain Andy did not consult me too much. My influence was only on the field and away from the games I was not any closer to Andy. The barrier was still there but I was determined to be non-confrontational, to walk away from situations which might have brought me into conflict with Andy or Craig Brown. It worked but it was something less than satisfactory even though we were praised for our performances. Mind you, we only won that single game against the CIS and lost to both Holland and Germany.

Last season I was sent off against Switzerland for deliberate handball in the 3-1 defeat there. I was suspended

and then injured and my next appearance – and my last –
was in Lisbon against Portugal. We lost disastrously – by
5-0 – and we should have lost by more. It could have been
an embarrassing double figures loss that night in the
Stadium of Light.

It was a shambles and it wasn't helped by the meetings
we had about the Portuguese team. Andy dismissed them.
They were crap, he told us. They were running scared. They
were afraid of us – now that was a little hard to believe
because we had just one win to our credit up to then and that
had arrived against Malta! He would always run down the
opposition, with Craig chipping in his remarks. Craig's
favourite was 'They all hate a heavy slap' – meaning they
didn't like to be tackled. I used to just about crack up at that
when you looked at the opposition. I think the first time he
used it was before an England game when he referred to
Chrissy Waddle and Glenn Hoddle that way. I was at Spurs
when he asked me to back up him and I just made the point
that you had to catch them first. It was always that way and
in Lisbon nothing had changed. The striker, Cadete, was
ordinary, he and Craig told me. I knew different because I
had seen him play on television and he had impressed me.
Then in the final team talk came the really good news from
the two of them. They knew the Portuguese team and they
knew that Rui Barros from Monaco would not be playing.
That allowed us to plan accordingly. They were delighted
with themselves. Then Craig Brown told us where he had
picked up this valuable information. It had come from a
Lisbon taxi driver!!

Think about that one – we did! It's like the Italian or the
Portuguese manager coming to Glasgow listening to a taxi
driver in the city and then planning a World Cup game
accordingly. Do you honestly think that would happen? I
don't – but it happened to Scotland.

The taxi driver's team was wrong, of course. We found that out when the teams were handed over half an hour before kick off – but the tactics were not changed. Rui Barros not only played but he scored their opening goal while we were still trying to adjust to the formation they were using. Rui Barros was running around unmarked – but then he wasn't playing, was he?

By the time I told Jim McInally to move into midfield from left-back the damage had been done. We were all over the place but when you examine the set-up you can understand why it turned into such a mess. Andy decided to play three at the back – myself, Dave McPherson and Craig Levein – with Craig marking Paulo Futre. Dave and I had been playing in a flat back four with Rangers all season and that had worked for us in Europe as well as at home. Now we were pitchforked into a different system. Stewart McKimmie was back after playing only a few matches following a four months long injury absence and Jim McInally was at left-back – he had played only part of a game since playing against Germany five weeks earlier. Yet they were handed the physically demanding wing back roles necessary in that set-up. When Jim moved in to mark Barros – which was essential – we were left with a gap on the left flank which they exploited.

As the game wore on nothing impoved. It was the worst night I had ever known in my career and yet at the end Andy came in and said almost nothing. No rollicking as you might have expected. It was as if he was shell-shocked. Then, of course, in the newspapers we read that a 'team has died in Lisbon', that things will have to change. After that some reports suggested that my career with my country was over. Andy didn't tell me this. But the journalists who wrote the stories remain convinced that his remarks at a Press Conference were hinting that I was finished.

Now if he had told me face to face, then fine. Team managers have to rebuild some time and you have to accept that. When I spoke to him he denied it all. Again the Pressmen were to blame though, this time, he had not read the reports.

I asked him if he would correct any misunderstandings there had been and he said he would. He didn't do it and that's when I made up my mind to pull out of international football as long as Andy Roxburgh remains in charge. This time I won't change my mind. I have been let down by the man too many times now.

Afterwards he criticised me for my timing – the timing of the remarks and the reluctance to set the record straight were down to him, not me. He also inferred that Ian Durrant had sent a message of support *after* I had announced I was quitting Scotland. Durranty has assured me that he sent no message and certainly *not* after my statement.

A lot of players – more than you might imagine – agree with me. They think that the team is run badly and we talk all the time among ourselves about the shambles it all is. If every player put his hand on his heart then they would tell you how ineffective the Roxburgh regime is. They won't do it because they want to keep on playing and I understand that. But I've had enough. More than enough!

I don't want to have to watch – as other players did – Craig Brown on his knees painting the white tapes around the front of Jim McInally's stockings because everyone has to look the same . . . and he was doing this before the team played Germany at Ibrox! It's trivial to players – it's vital to Craig and Andy. Maybe that's why John Brown hasn't played for Scotland – because he uses these tapes too.

Nor do I want to have to rehearse the new set-up at the National Anthem. Craig now wants players to stand with their hand resting on the next player's shoulder. He introduced this at the Under-21 tournament in Toulon and had the players rehearsing it in the dressing-room before an important match. Again – does it matter?

Sadly for Andy and Craig these pieces of trivia and all the team meetings assume an importance that the players find laughable. I'm just glad that I won't have to sit through another team meeting. Or listen to another taxi driver's tactics. It's over and I'm glad. I just worry about where the Scotland team is heading under the present managerial set-up.

CHAPTER THREE

The £1.5m Scenic Route to Ibrox

It took me more than seven years and eventually cost Rangers £1.5 million before I was able to make my schoolboy ambitions come true and join up at Ibrox.

Growing up in South Africa, the talk was always about football around my house. My father had played as a professional with Charlton Athletic and had then moved to Johannesburg. He played there and he managed a team there and inevitably there were football people around all the time as I was growing up. Just as inevitably a lot of the players and ex-players were Scottish and so I heard story after story about the game back home. Lots of these stories concerned Rangers as one of the ex-players who visited was Don Kichenbrand. I suppose it was then, all those thousands of miles away, that Ibrox became my own personal field of dreams. So many of the tales which were told revolved around games at Ibrox or Hampden Park, around Old Firm games and European games and those clashes with England when they were so vitally important to the Scots.

They fired my imagination. My Dad's friends told me of the passion for the game in Glasgow, the huge gates at the games, and while other youngsters might have been thinking of English football I have to say that Scottish football meant more to me then. And Rangers, in particular, became the team I wanted to play for.

We all have those childhood dreams. Thousands of youngsters in Scotland still dream just the way I did. But their hopes and ambitions must seem more attainable . . . mine were half a world away. But distance did not diminish them.

What I did not realise back then – and there was no way that I could ever have visualised the roundabout road I had to take to get to Rangers – was how difficult it would be to sign for the club Don Kichenbrand and others had told me so much about. Nor did I have any idea how defeated I was going to feel after my first chance to train with the club I now captain. That came on my third attempt to break into football in Britain. In South Africa I was fortunate to be at a primary school, King Edward, which had a strong sports background and which encouraged soccer over rugby. Gary Bailey, who played for Manchester United, went to that school and so did my best friend from schooldays, Mitch D'Avray, who had a long career with Ipswich Town in their glory days when Bobby Robson was their manager.

It was at Ipswich I had my first opportunity to try out for a professional club. By that time I had moved on to Highland School, where rugby was the game which was played. That was compulsory and so I began playing rugby for the school in the mornings and soccer for youth teams in the afternoons every single Saturday in life. By the time I was 14 I was being selected for representative teams and so I was following my first love and finding some encouragment in the game. A year later, when we were both 15 years old, Mitch and myself were invited to go over to Ipswich for training and trials in the summer.

By now the Rangers influence around the house had grown. Bobby Hume and Craig Watson, both ex-Ibrox men, were playing there and both were friends of my dad. He had been there since 1965 or 1966 and had played and managed in South Africa. They would come to him for advice or help but while they talked about Rangers there were never suggestions that I might go there. So I went to Ipswich!

Not that I lasted too long there. I was told I was too small and to maybe return the following summer. Mitch was signed and he stayed there for a long time and had a successful career – but, at 15, after a month's trial I was packed off back home to South Africa. It was no one's fault because I was small at 15 and Ipswich did not want to commit themselves.

Bobby Robson was the manager then and I remember the day I scored the winner for Scotland against England at Hampden when he was international team boss. I said to him after the game: 'You won't remember me but I came over for trials with Mitch D'Avray all those years ago . . .' And he told me that he did remember but I hadn't returned the following summer when he had given me that invitation.

Then, a couple of years back, Mitch had a Testimonial and I was down there and at the dinner afterwards Bobby Robson told the story again. He started off his speech by saying: 'I can still remember the day that Mitch arrived with his friend from South Africa. These two little lads had both been recommended to me and I decided to keep Mitch but let the other one go back home because he was so small. I should have kept them both because the other lad was Richard Gough!'

We had a laugh about it then and a chat and there was no doubt that he did remember. And I did too because I felt the door was shutting on a football career for me. That feeling was heightened because Mitch had been asked to sign and his future was mapped out in the game. Mine was on hold and I went back to playing in South Africa, not really believing that I could make the grade in Britain.

By the time the next summer arrived I had grown a bit and I had also moved up a grade in the South African game. I had made my senior debut with Witz University where a former Manchester United player, Eddie Lewis, was coaching. My Dad reckoned that he was the best guide for young players. He had come out to South Africa in 1971 after a spell with West Ham as well as his time at Old Trafford. He reckoned that I should give it another go in Britain, but under his influence – and some input from my Dad – I decided against returning to Ipswich even though Mitch was happy there.

Eddie Lewis had a couple of good pals who were with Charlton and my Dad had played there and that gave The Valley extra appeal for me. The club knew him and so it gave me a little bit more of an 'in' if you like and after a few weeks training with them they offered me a deal. They wanted me to sign a two- or a three-year contract and I eventually agreed a two-year deal. But within a few months I was desperately unhappy and homesick. I had come from a home in South Africa with a swimming pool in the backyard and where the sun shone all the time and now I was in digs looking out of the window at rain and a view of the docks. It was not a good environment and, while I stuck it out for six months or so trying my best to adjust, things became worse and worse, I knew this was not for me and after seven months of my contract I went in to see the manager, a man called Andy Nelson, and told him I had to get back home. He saw the problems I was facing, understood them and agreed to release me from my contract. I doubt if I'll ever be able to thank him enough for the kindness he showed me then. It was marvellous to be going home and it was a bonus that he had let me go without having the complications a valid contract would have given me.

The contract had been as an apprentice professional and it was intended to run until I was 17 and then, if they had wanted, Charlton would have given me a full professional agreement. This was around February or March of 1979 and all I wanted was to get back home and look at some other kind of career. I was more or less convinced, by this time, that professional football was not for me. Still, I did not want to stop playing altogether and so I went back to my old club and my old coach, Eddie Lewis, and began playing with them again. In fact, I had a full season with them as a semi-professional and in that time I began to develop physically. Inside a year I had grown several inches, I had filled out and, generally, matured. It was then that my Dad took a hand in things. He thought that I had a chance to make it in the professional game and urged me to try again. I wasn't wildly enthusiastic but I listened to him and I looked at a couple of opportunities which came up. One was a soccer scholarship in the United States at the University of Miami – and though soccer seemed to be taking off around that time I didn't fancy that.

The other was to go to Sweden for trials. Since my mother came from Stockholm and I had been born there, this had its attractions. Mind you, my being born in Sweden was a little bit of an accident. My Dad had been in the army and had been sent out to the Middle East after marrying my mother, who was a nurse near the barracks at Aldershot where he was stationed. I was due to be born while he was on a tour of duty in Bahrain and rather than be on her own my mother flew to Stockholm to be with her parents. My Dad preferred that to having me born an Englishman! I was only there a couple of months before going to Britain.

Anyhow, that brief period, plus the fact that my place of birth was given as Stockholm, alerted a couple of guys who had been coaching in South Africa but had just moved to Sweden. One was Bobby Houghton, who did so well with Malmo eventually, and his right-hand man was Roy Hodgson – who came into my life again recently as the team boss of Switzerland who damaged Scotland's World Cup dreams so badly in our first qualifying match for the 1994 USA finals. They knew me – as a player – from their own time working in South Africa and they knew my Dad. Given the Swedish connection, slight though it was, they believed that they could tempt me to join them there.

It was here that my Dad stepped in again. He didn't want me to go there and, in fact, he had now made up his mind that he would like me to try my luck in Scotland. Don Kichenbrand was working for him and he recommended me to Rangers. He spoke to Willie Thornton at Ibrox and arranged that I should train with Rangers and let them have first look at me. As well as that chance Joe Gilroy, who had played in South Africa, had spoken to Jim McLean at Dundee United and Alex Ferguson at Aberdeen and they had also agreed to give me trials. Joe had been a team-mate of Jim McLean at Clyde and had then played for my Dad's club in South Africa. It was then arranged that I would fly to Glasgow, stay with Joe Gilroy in Newton Mearns, and kick off my bid to launch a career in Scottish football at Ibrox. It was an exciting prospect – I just didn't realise the let-down I was about to suffer.

I arrived at the end of February 1980 just before my 18th birthday knowing deep down that this was my third – and probably last chance of carving out a career in professional football for myself. I trained for a few days, then I played in a game at Lesser Hampden and I thought I had done really well. But the back-room guys who were with the club then didn't agree. Now, I had been playing in the First Division back in South Africa and that was a pretty decent standard and I knew I was as good if not better than any of the other lads I was playing alongside in that match, and I wasn't kidding myself on. I *knew* that I had played well. After that the manager, it was John Greig at the time, called me in and told me that they had three or four young players who played in the same position as I did and that they would be sticking with them. That meant there was no chance of a contract for Yours Truly. John is back at Ibrox now and the lads sometimes kid him about letting me go and the club having to buy me back for £1.5 million. But the reality is that John had been away with the first-team squad and hadn't seen me play. He acted on the assessments from his back-room staff and those opinions said I was not good enough.

I remember going back downstairs at Ibrox thinking, I've come all this way dreaming of playing for this club and it's over. The dream had ended and I would soon be flying back to South Africa with the news for my Dad that I had not been good enough to sign for Glasgow Rangers. You would not believe how disappointed I felt – and that disappointment was all the greater because I knew that I was good enough. If I had performed badly in that game, then I would not have felt so let down. But deep down, I reckoned that I had not been judged fairly by the people in charge of the side that day. I thought that the least I deserved was another chance. To a large extent I had set my heart on joining Rangers. I knew my Dad wanted me to join them too. And, after all, they were the team I had heard so much about, the biggest team in Scotland.

I had been at Ibrox just a week and I can still remember some of the players who were there. Tom Forsyth, Derek Johnstone, Alex MacDonald and John McDonald were in the first team then. Funnily enough, none of the players who were considered better than me then lasted the course. I can't remember who they were, but I know they weren't around Ibrox when I eventually did sign for the club. Strange that, isn't it?

Leaving Ibrox that day, I can still remember thinking to myself that if I was not good enough for Rangers then it was doubtful if anyone else would want to take a chance on me. But I thought I would go up to Dundee United, give it a whirl there and then try out at Aberdeen before heading home. I travelled to Dundee with no great expectations. In fact one of the reasons I decided to go to Dundee was that another friend of my Dad, Billy McLardy – who is still a friend of mine to this day – had offered to put me up. He had played in South Africa for my Dad's team so I thought it would be good to see him again and take my chances with Dundee United at the same time. Then I would head on up to Aberdeen and get myself back home and explain to my dad that I wasn't good enough. He would have been disappointed but I knew he would accept it if I had given myself every chance to impress the clubs I had trial arrangements with.

Anyhow, my first stop after Ibrox was Tannadice and after a few days training Jim McLean put me into a reserve game down at Arbroath. I played left-back at Gayfield that day and the man who is now my Boss, Walter Smith, was at centre-back. I didn't think I did particularly well but by now I was so sure that I would be going home without a contract I wasn't too bothered. The Ibrox let-down was sinking in now. But, as they say, it's a funny old game, football. After that match Jim McLean offered me a one-year contract. I phoned my Dad back home. He told me to sign it and that was that. I never did make it up to Aberdeen.

I found myself going straight into the reserve team and Walter Smith was my playing partner at centre-back. I became very close to Walter then. He was finishing his playing career. Basically, he was in charge of the reserve team and playing as well and, besides that, he used to come and pick me up in the morning and drive me into training. It was a real learning process for me then and Walter was one of the main teachers. It was easy to learn from him by playing with him. I had almost a whole year doing that. It was my apprenticeship, before making my debut in April 1981 just before my 19th birthday. I went on against Celtic as a sub and the following season I had become more or less a first-team regular – though I was without a regular position. I was used in midfield, at full-back and sometimes, though not often, in a central defensive role. I wasn't played there because Paul Hegarty and Dave Narey held down those positions back then and they *were* Dundee United. They were the twin pillars wee Jim built his great team of the eighties upon. And so my favourite position wasn't available and I was moved around. Now I realise how valuable that was for me as a learning experience. I also grew to realise that while my heart had always said Rangers when I thought of where I wanted to play, that perhaps Dundee United would give me a better start. Rangers were going through a troubled spell while United were strong contenders for the major honours – and were already respected right across Europe as a tactically sound team. As a learning ground I was probably at the best place possible in Scotland.

That didn't stop me walking out and heading off home again, though. Around Christmas 1981 homesickness hit me pretty hard. I spoke to Walter about it first because, by now, we were close and he was the man I went to for advice. He tried to talk me out of it but once I have something in my mind then I'm pretty hard to budge. Basically I can be stubborn. I told him that I wanted to go home, that I didn't want to pursue a career in football any longer and I wanted to do something else with my life. And that life was going to be in South Africa. Walter was furious with me. He could not understand that I was ready to give up all I had worked for up to that time. He went in to see the manager and told him. He hoped that Jim McLean would convince me to stay.

McLean certainly tried – but he didn't make an impression on me at all. I still recall going into his office and sitting there while both he and Walter tried to persuade me to stay at Tannadice. I can still hear wee Jim telling me: 'If you keep playing football and keep working and improving the way you are doing then you are going to be playing for Scotland one day very soon!'

I could scarcely believe that. In fact, at the time, I thought he was talking rubbish, that he was exaggerating just to get me to stay on. I was hardly in the United first team and here he was talking about international honours. It was only later I realised that he had meant what he said and that it had not been just a ploy to get me to stay. Then, however, it was hard for me to take in, especially as I had my heart set on a return home and a career in the army along with some of my former schoolmates.

I realised that this was not going to be as simple as leaving Charlton because, by now, I was on one of wee Jim's famous long-term contracts – three years plus option years – and he told me that I would be held to that. In essence that meant that I would not be able to play football in any other country which was in membership of FIFA. That did not upset me as much as Jim McLean had hoped because back then South Africa was not affiliated to football's governing body and so I could go back to playing semi-professional soccer there if I wanted to. Mind you, that was not uppermost in my plans.

I had been speaking to my mates on the phone all the time and the Army seemed to be a reasonable prospect. When I did get home it was to the warmest of welcomes. My dad didn't say too much but he made it pretty obvious that he was far from happy at my decision to give up the game. Anyhow I went of to Durban to see some of my friends who had been in the army and I very quickly found out that things were not as rosy as they had seemed when I was back in Dundee. Some of my pals had been wounded in border skirmishes and when I spoke to them and thought it all through it didn't take me long to realise that playing football for a living – even though it was far from home – wasn't such a bad career prospect.

By now Jim McLean had been on the phone to my Dad every day or two trying to get him to talk me into returning to Tannadice. Eventually I spoke to him and he said that he would pay my fare back and write off the absence as a holiday. I had been away for six weeks and then took up his offer – within a few days of being back I was playing in the first team again. It was almost as if he was determined to reassure me that I had done the right thing, that my future was in football, and my immediate future was with Dundee United.

If I remember correctly I got back to Dundee on a Saturday, obviously missed the game which was played that day, but was in the team at Love Street the following Tuesday night. I played in midfield as we lost 1-0 to St Mirren to a goal scored by Frank McAvennie. From then – February 1982 – I was a regular in the first team until I was transferred.

Looking back now I find it hard to explain why I went home like that. Staying in digs far from home isn't the easiest thing to adjust to and a whole lot of events just seemed to get on top of me. I just felt very low – even though the football was fine. In fact it was going better than I could have hoped. But I still felt restless and unsettled and my own impulsiveness when added to that suddenly saw me on the plane home. I have always been strong-minded and when I get something in my head then I usually go for it. This time I had made up my mind that football was not the career I wanted and so I turned my back on Dundee United. I ignored good advice from Walter Smith and Jim McLean and went my own way. And I was wrong.

Indeed Jim McLean's international prophecy began to turn into reality just six weeks or so after I came home. The late Jock Stein, then Scotland manager, selected me for the Scotland Under-21 squad and I went on in that first game as a substitute. I have always had a sneaking feeling that wee Jim told Jock Stein that I had dual nationality and could play for Sweden if they decided to pick me. He got in first and made certain that I would be a Scotland player in the future – though I wanted to play for Scotland in any case. I'd only been born in Stockholm, after all, because my Dad didn't want me born in England and if I had chosen to play for anyone other than Scotland he would have killed me!

That six weeks' break helped concentrate my mind on the career I had now decided without any doubts was for me. My early education with Dundee United was something I needed. I had a natural athleticism which is important in the modern game and I had enthusiasm but at Tannadice I was played in different positions and learned so much tactically. Wee Jim finally had me settle down at right-back. He believed that I possessed a goal threat and he believed, too, that if you could get defenders to score goals then that was a bonus for any team. He liked me to get forward. He wanted me to get into the opposition penalty box and get on the end of things there. I was good in the air and as well as pushing into attacking positions he had me upfield for set pieces. I was able to get double figures, or very nearly, in goals for the seasons he played me there.

These were good times, too, to be with United. I watched from the terraces, still a reserve player, as they won the League Cup against Dundee at Dens Park in 1980. Two years later they would win the Premier League title and in the time I was there United were on a high. It may have been a small club – but it was a powerful club in a playing sense. In the four years I was there in the first team we took a lot of scalps and were one of the most consistent teams in Scotland. Apart from the domestic successes the team was also respected in Europe. We had a reputation far ahead of bigger teams in Britain. Honestly, it was a good place to learn my trade and a good place to taste success for the first time.

But there came a time when I knew I had to move on and it was that decision which soured my relationship with Jim McLean. Since then, back in 1986, he and I have not been on the best of terms. And that is putting it mildly!

Before the World Cup finals in Mexico in 1986 Rangers had sparked off what has now come to be known as the 'Souness revolution'. They had appointed Graeme Souness as Ibrox manager and taken Walter Smith from Tannadice as his assistant. One of the earliest moves the new management pairing made was to make a bid for my transfer. They offered Dundee United £650,000 and I hoped that United would consider selling me and, hoped, too, that my future could be settled before Scotland went to the finals in Mexico. I didn't want to be heading off there with my future undecided. Jim McLean, being Jim McLean, of course, was as stubborn as you would have expected him to be. Rangers were told I was not for sale and then when I returned for the new season he told me that he was insisting that I see out my full contract. Again it was a McLean special, a long-term deal which tied me to the club until 1990.

Yet, I was prepared to stay if United had been willing to match their valuation of me in the transfer market in salary. I thought that if they thought I was such a huge asset – close to three quarters of a million pounds – then I should be paid accordingly. That was a piece of logic which, of course, was lost on the manager.

I could understand that United did not want to sell me to Rangers who were local rivals in the Scottish game. I had to accept this, although the move was one I wanted because I could sense that a new order was coming and that Graeme and Walter were going to turn the game around. That is what happened but I had to watch the beginnings of that revolution from a distance.

What I could not understand was why United refused to sell me at all and yet would not pay me the kind of salary I could expect to earn elsewhere. It struck me as selfish and small-minded. Yet, even though I sensed that United were never going to give me any kind of satisfaction I still tried everything in an effort to find a solution to the problem. If they had agreed to my suggestion to end the stalemate then I might still be a Tannadice player. I asked for a single payment of £50,000 and guaranteed that I would see out my contract with the club. The chairman then was George Fox and I went to his home in Carnoustie to discuss the matter with him. I explained to him my view of the situation that if I was worth a huge sum of money to the club then I was worth the kind of money I could earn elsewhere. When I finished the talks and left his home that night I was certain that I had convinced him that my arguments were right. Mr Fox had given me a decent hearing, had listened to what I had to say and had admitted that there was some merit in what I was saying. I was sure that he would recommend to the board that I should be paid a lump sum and that I would then fulfil my lengthy contract. I was wrong. Not for the first time I had under-estimated the power that Jim McLean had at the club.

The next day I was called in front of the board and told that I would not be allowed to leave. A written request I had made for a transfer before I had tried to resolve things was rejected. I was back where I had started and I was less than happy with the way the board had handled things.

There is no doubt that it was the manager who had opposed my suggestion of a lump sum payment. He was vehemently against my getting any fresh deal while I was still under contract. His view – an absolutely unshakeable view – was that any new arrangement for me would upset the wage structure at the club. He also suggested that if I was to get extra cash this would upset some of the more senior players and therefore United would have to pay out more money to them at a time when the club could not afford to do so.

It won't come as any surprise to you that I did not see things that way at all. As far as I was concerned it was up to each individual player to make his own deal with the club. If they wanted more money they should ask for it – if they got it then that was good for them. Maybe, of course, some of them had already asked and been refused but that was none of my business. Maybe they were happy with whatever they were earning with Dundee United at that time – again, that was none of my business. In my case Dundee United had more or less put a huge price on my head and they were going to make hundreds of thousands of pounds for a player who had cost them practically nothing. To put it simply, my argument was then – as it is now – that if I was worth all that money to the club if I was transferred then I was worth a bigger wage deal from them.

I honestly felt that I had been fair to Dundee United but, by now, I doubted very much if they had been fair to me. Around the time all this was going on it had come out in the newspapers that several other clubs had made offers for me at one time or another. They had all been told that I was happy to stay where I was. Whether that was true or not didn't come into things as far as Jim McLean was concerned. He made up my mind for me. That was not right. It is not the way a player should be treated. Essentially I saw it as dishonest and unfair. It cannot be right that a player in these circumstances has no say at all in his future – and we are talking in my case of a future which was going to be much more lucrative and much more secure than the one on offer at Tannadice.

This time was different from the others, however. Because this time I knew that a bid had been made by Rangers and that now another had been made by Spurs. It was common knowledge.

That is what made up my mind that I had now to do something drastic to bring things to a head. I had tried to play the diplomat with the chairman George Fox – and that had failed me. What Jim McLean failed to realise was that the outcome of these talks had failed him too. Because of his intransigence I now knew that I had to move. I had to get away from Dundee United – and yet for £50,000 I would have agreed to stay there for at least another four years. Now that had been knocked back – blocked by the manager – I recognised that this was going to be a battle of wills. It was a personal clash between myself and the manager and I was utterly determined that I was not going to lose!

There were two things that were going to work in my favour in the dispute. The first was that United could not really afford to turn their backs on £650,000 and the second was that South Africa remained outlawed by FIFA and if I decided to go back there and play semi-professional football there was nothing that Dundee United, Jim McLean, the SFA or FIFA could do about it. Nothing at all.

Jim McLean knew that too because when I first signed he had used it to his advantage. My club back in South Africa had asked United for a fee. They had been given a goodwill payment from Manchester United when Gary Bailey joined up at Old Trafford and thought the same would apply to my move. It didn't. Wee Jim relied on the fact that South Africa was not a member of FIFA and therefore the club were not entitled to a penny. So they got nothing – and that wasn't because United had lavished money on me. I signed for sweeties and that was one of the reasons I was now digging my heels in. I really felt that United owed me for the four very good years I had given them. If they would not pay me and they refused to transfer me I would just go home.

I would have done it too. It would have meant giving up all I had managed to build up for myself in football. I would have had to turn my back on international football after playing in the World Cup finals. I would have had to give up the dreams I had of playing for a bigger club and winning still more honours. But this was a matter of principle as well as a personal issue between myself and Jim McLean and I was not bluffing. I would have caught a plane back to South Africa and picked up the threads of my life there. It would not have been easy but I felt it was something I had to be prepared to do – and Jim McLean knew me well enough to accept that I was a man of my word.

He was left with the worry over losing a top player *and* losing the huge amount of money he was to have brought in when he was transferred. He was facing a bigger dilemma than I was. That, if you like, was my ace card. Fortunately it never came to the crunch, but if it had then I would have been on a plane back to South Africa. And, no doubt, when I got there I would have been met with a message telling me to return to Britain as the club had accepted an offer for my transfer.

When I think back I often come to the conclusion that I could still be a United player today if things had been handled better by the manager. Instead our relationship ended then. It has never been the same since I dug in my heels and made it clear that I was determined to leave. I would have forgiven and forgotten because that's my way. Sadly Jim won't let go of an issue. He worries at it, gnaws at it all the time, and seems to grow more and more bitter. I was bad-mouthed and criticised and, at the end of it all, as far as I'm concerned, Jim McLean did not carry out his duties as a manager. When the club finally agreed to let me go it wasn't the manager who spoke to me about the two clubs who were interested.

Spurs had been first on the scene with an offer and then Chelsea arrived late to match that bid. I learned all of this from one of the directors who phoned me on a Saturday night at 11 o'clock to say I had to fly to London the following day. The director was the late George Grant, a gentleman, and I asked him why the manager was not telling me of these developments. He told me: 'The manager does not want to speak to you about any of this. He told the directors that he did not want to be involved in the transfer once the fee we wanted had been met by the interested clubs. That's why I have had to call you.'

I was furious that he should treat me like this. I knew what he was saying about me behind my back and I knew he was far from happy at the way I had stood up to him – though he was delighted with the money he was going to get for the club. Because I was so upset I phoned Jim McLean after speaking to George Grant. Initially I was going to tell him I had something else on and could not fly down to London the following day. Then I thought that, instead, I would talk to him about the two clubs who were in for me and ask him for his advice on which one I should join.

It was a wind-up, pure and simple. I was just getting back at him because I knew he had washed his hands of the transfer even though his job demanded that he see it through. He took it seriously and went about criticising me again for daring to ask his advice. But it was never a serious phone call. Jim should have known that one thing I was good at was making up my own mind! The problem, of course, was that Jim doesn't really have much of a sense of humour. He could not even see that I was just noising him up in retaliation for his attitude to me.

I signed for Spurs that Sunday and pushed Jim McLean and his attitude towards me into the back of my mind. But even while I was pursuing a new career at White Hart Lane he could not leave me alone. After a particularly good win in Europe for United – I think it was against Barcelona – he took another silly swipe at me. It was around the time we had lost in the League Cup semi-final to Arsenal and United were going strongly in the UEFA Cup, so after the game he decided to have a go at me. He also criticised Davie Dodds, but I was called 'selfish' among other things. I could not believe it. His job was to look after the players he had. His future and Dundee United's future was with them – yet here he was complaining about me more than six months after I had gone. It was bizarre and I phoned him to ask if the quotes attributed to him were correct. He said they were. I told him that they were a disgrace and put down the phone. That is the last conversation I had with him.

If we are playing at Tannadice or United are at Ibrox and I see him I'll say, 'Hello', but that's all. It never goes beyond that. I am certainly not on his Christmas card list but I have long since stopped caring about that. He caused the trouble between us. Not me. He made sure that the trouble continued between us. Not me.

Recently I did get myself involved in the row he had with Rangers over Duncan Ferguson when he was talking about the player being 'tapped'. All I did then was simply tell the truth that he had once asked me to tap a player for him. It was my mate from South Africa, Mitch D'Avray, he wanted me to speak to. A dozen other players could probably tell similar stories. The trouble with Jim McLean is that he sees things only from his own viewpoint. You would think, by this time, he would realise there are occasions when even he can be wrong.

Even when I returned to Rangers from Tottenham Hotspur he insisted to people that it had all been a set-up, that I had gone to London knowing that I would return to Rangers just as soon as possible. This was arrant nonsense.

It was true that given the chance I would have gone to Rangers directly from Dundee United. They were the first club in for me, after all. But Jim McLean insisted from the start that he would not sell me to Ibrox under any circumstances and that was that.

When Spurs came on the scene I was happy to go there because they were a big club and an ambitious club. But after initial good times my wife Lesley became homesick. She wanted to go back to Scotland because she wanted to be closer to her mother and, naturally, she was going to take my son Michael back with her. It was a major problem for us and there was no obvious solution.

So, in October 1987, more than seven years after my first attempt to join Rangers, I signed for them. Graeme Souness paid £1.5 million to get me away from Spurs. It was a huge amount of money and the fact that they had picked up double what they had paid for me little over a year earlier must have been some consolation to Spurs.

My consolation, apart from the personal aspects of the move – the family problems were now solved – was that I was finally signing for Rangers. The club which had rejected me when I first arrived from South Africa had now paid a record club price to sign me. You can imagine all of that running through my mind as I arrived and went up the marble staircase to the manager's office.

The last time I had made that journey it had ended in the biggest disappointment of my life. I had been told that I was not good enough to play for the team I had desperately wanted to join. This time they wanted me and I felt that I had achieved one of my ambitions and maybe one of my Dad's ambitions too. It was certainly something for me to celebrate and I knew that there would be a few people back in South Africa who would be toasting the transfer too. The guys who had kindled my imagination with stories of great Rangers teams would be happy that I had now joined the club. And happier still at the direction the club was moving in. It had been a long wait but it was to turn out to be something worth waiting for.

CHAPTER FOUR

Tannadice – Triumphs and Tribulations

My time at Tannadice may have ended in tears but there were good times there too. So many, many good times because back then United were a force to be reckoned with. I was lucky to move into such a talented team. While Jim McLean may not believe it, I know that I owe him and the club and the other players there a lot.

I said in the last chapter that Rangers were not at their best when I came to Scotland for the first time and if I had been given my first opportunity there instead of at Tannadice then I don't know how my future might have been. I'd like to think that I would have come through OK – then I remember the other young players who were rated higher than I was and I wonder where all of them ended up.

At Tannadice I was given a grounding in the game which enabled me to make the most of what ability I had and allowed me to develop as a footballer. Certainly I would not have made such rapid progress if I had gone to Rangers. I might still have been toiling away in the reserves there – if they had kept me – when, with United, I was pushing my way into the Scotland Under-21 team. The fact that the club was on such a high around that time undoubtedly helped me on a personal level. If you look back at the record they had in the four years or so that I was a part of the first team then you will be able to relate to what I am saying here. In that spell we reached the final of the Scottish Cup once, the final of the League Cup once, the semi-finals of the European Cup and we won the Premier League title – a first for the club. These were incredible achievements for a club as small as United. I doubt if they will ever be repeated. And just to underline the astonishing consistency the club showed during those years we finished in third spot in the Premier League for the three years following our title win.

As well as that run of success and near success at home, we navigated our way through Europe with a style which suited the two-legged games you played in the Continental competitions. The club's battle honours over the years carry some notable results and while that may surprise some people today – just as it did the various foreign sides then – it was a record founded on solid football principles. The manager had put together a strong back four – he had myself now at right-back, Paul Hegarty and Dave Narey as central defenders and Maurice Malpas at left-back. It was a strong and disciplined unit and eventually became experienced at both club and international level. Up front he put Ralph Milne and Paul Sturrock who were both very, very quick. They were used on the break. We would play the ball up to Paul Sturrock and he would hold it and keep possession until we could get players up in support. It was a case of either myself or some of the midfield players moving up to join him – it was a tactic which worked superbly well for the club, particularly in the European ties.

It happens at times that clubs have a golden period when players peak at the same time. When a crop of good players arrives and then they work together and train together and play together and, to some extent, grow up together. That happened during those years at Tannadice. Jim McLean had experienced players in the team – Hamish McAlpine in goal, Hegarty and Narey and Eamonn Bannon and then David Dodds and Paul Sturrock up front. Then there was the younger element – myself, Maurice Malpas, Billy Kirkwood and Ralphie Milne.

My later problems with Jim McLean have never blinded me to the fact that he could spot a player. He has the ability to look at a youngster and recognise in that raw talent something – I don't know what it is – which will eventually flower into real ability. He was able to spot whether a player had the character or the skill or the football brain to make it all the way as a professional. You have only to look at the teams he produced and the home-grown talent which graced so many of them to realise that. Other aspects of his management style can leave something to be desired but that initial recognition of talent is a special gift and he has it.

David Narey was a great player – and still is. He has looked after himself and even after losing a year out of his career quite recently because of a back injury he remains an influential figure in the United defence. Davie won 35 caps for Scotland but they arrived over a 12-year period and he deserved to have so many more. Unfortunately he was playing at the same time and in the same position as Willie Miller and Alan Hansen and some of his caps were won in positions which were not his best. He was a very talented player, intelligent in defence and just as intelligent in his use of the ball. On the Continent he would have been a sensation as a 'sweeper'. Here at home he was one of the unsung heroes during the glory years at Tannadice.

Hamish McAlpine was often undervalued too – probably because he was one of the great goalkeeping eccentrics. He drove Jim crazy at times with his antics but today Hamish would be a sensation playing with the new pass back rule. That was made for him. If he had been drafting the new rules then he could not have done better than the change in the pass back situation. It would have been food and drink to Hamish.

He came before his time as far as the new set up is concerned. Our 'keeper at Ibrox, Andy Goram, has adapted to the change superbly. Hamish would have been the same. He would have revelled in the whole thing. I mean, back when I played with him at Tannadice, it was a regular occurrence for Hamish to come out of goal and start dribbling the ball past opposition forwards. That's the kind of thing which used to have wee Jim going mental in the dugout. But he was good at it, so good that he was used almost as another sweeper by United. His use of the ball from hand, too, was magnificent. He could start attacks with his throw-outs or even by coming out of the penalty box and placing passes upfield – just as Andy does at Ibrox now. Like Andy he had a great eye and perfect timing. Andy's success at cricket has demonstrated that while Hamish was a scratch golfer. Again, like Andy, he was not big for a 'keeper but he had a good eye and the way he always tried to use the ball when he was making a clearance was an extra shot in our locker at that time. No one really gave Hamish enough credit.

It was the same with Ralph Milne who, for me, was a lost talent. He and I were very friendly but I'm not talking through that friendship when I say that Ralphie was one of the biggest tragedies in the Scottish game. He was a flying machine when he was at his best. No one in Scotland could come close to matching him for pace. He was also a lethal finisher but somehow he was never able to put all of that together and reach a consistency of performance. You have to be able to do that. You must be able to turn it on week after week, game after game. Doing it only when you feel like doing it just doesn't work any longer. The modern game demands more than that from players – sadly Ralphie couldn't give it all the time.

The problem Ralph had was Jim McLean. He had a lot of troubles with him before he was sold to Charlton and while some were his own fault, others were not. Certain players require to be handled in certain ways. It's not possible to treat everyone the same. You have different natures and they will throw up different reactions but wee Jim never saw that. He didn't subscribe to the fact that some players might have to be coaxed a little instead of being threatened. As far as he was concerned a player was a player and they all got the same tongue-lashings in the dressing-room. But that was not the way to deal with Ralph Milne. He needed someone to boost his confidence – wee Jim destroyed it. The last thing Ralph needed was some one barking at him all the time, blaming him whenever things didn't go the way they were supposed to go. That made Ralph withdraw. He turned into a frightened player, someone who was scared to take defenders on, who was scared to try a shot – because he knew if he failed he would be hammered by the manager. When Ralph's confidence was high he could be a world beater. No doubt it will be said that I'm biased because he is a mate. But ask any player who was at Tannadice then and they will tell you just how good Ralph Milne might have been. He would have been a wonderful player at club and at international level.

By the time he left Tannadice his confidence was shattered. He had that spell with Charlton and then Fergie gave him a chance at Manchester United but, by then, he had lost the sparkle he had as a young player. It was a tragedy. He was someone who should have been an international regular – he never even won a single cap. He was not the most disciplined lad I've known and he battled with weight problems during his career, but handed some encouragement at the right times he would have been a class act.

Jim, though, would not change for anyone. He had one way of ruling the dressing-room and that was by fear. He would abuse players and insult them and he would fine them if they stepped out of line. In fact, he would often fine you even when you hadn't stepped out of line. A below par performance could cost you money and while it did bring success there were times when I felt he would have got even more from the players if only he could have lightened up a little. That was never his way and his way at Tannadice was the only way!

Apart from disagreeing with the way he handled some of the players – Ralph Milne is just one outstanding example – I often wonder how much his attitude to life coloured the displays of the team. He was so downbeat that you often found that coming across in his tactics. Jim would always err on the side of caution. He was unhappy if the team went into all-out attack – he always wanted men to stay back in numbers. I can still remember a row with him at Motherwell in my last season there. We were aiming for the League and Cup double that season for a long, long time. Then we lost to Hearts in the semi-final of the Scottish Cup and we lost crucial Premier League games on the run-in as well. That was the year Celtic pipped Hearts for the title and we had faded to third place after running the two other contenders desperately close for most of the season.

Anyhow, this day at Fir Park we were still involved in the title race and we had to win. But, for whatever reason, wee Jim had opted for a defensive set up. Ralph Milne was playing at outside-right and he was constantly dropping back to a position right in front of me at right-back. On the other side of the field Davie Dodds was dropping back just as deep. Here we were in a game we had to win and we had two attacking players spending more time in their own half than in their opponents' half.

At the interval we were trailing 1-0 and while I had been trying to get Ralphie to go further upfield he was stopped all the time by Jim screaming at him to 'Get back, get back . . .' None of this made any sense to me and I said so in the dressing-room at half time. My comments made no difference on the day – it was just another mark against me in wee Jim's black book. I was wrong to try to make my point and doing so did me no favours at all with him. Yet this was a game I knew we could win and if we had done so we would have remained in the frame with Hearts at the top. At the end of the game we had lost 2-0 and our chances of winning the title again had lessened – just as my chances of being wee Jim's favourite player had also lessened. I spoke out because I sensed we could win the game if we were that little bit bolder – but Jim could never see things that way. If he could win games and still be that little bit careful in defence then he was a happy man – or as happy as he can be.

That row was towards the end of my time with the club and I was beginning to realise by then just how much Jim's attitudes affected the side. From a distance I can see that even more clearly now. Just look back at all the finals Dundee United have been in – and the semi-finals at Hampden too – and look at how often they have failed. That has to tell you something. It cannot all be down to a Hampden jinx. It cannot all be down to bad luck because it has happened too often. And it has happened even when United have been favourites to win the games. After I left they were in Scottish Cup finals against St Mirren and

Motherwell. No one could see past them. Each time was going to be the day when wee Jim finally won the Cup. Each time they blew it. Honestly, I put most of the failures down to his basically negative approach to the game. That has definitely damaged them down through the years.

At Tannadice the team was always organised with defence the first priority. It was not just the back four wee Jim worked with when he was laying down the tactics, it was the midfield who had to close people down before they could get at the back line. And it was the forwards, too, who had to check back into defensive areas. That's the way it was whenever we were away from home, with Ralph Milne and Davie Dodds dropping so deep they were standing on the full-backs' toes. It's always been my belief that defenders should defend, midfielders should play in their areas and that attackers should stay where they can cause most damage to the opposition. That's in the other team's half of the field and not your own. But with United everyone had to get behind the ball, everyone had to be trying to mark other players out of the game, with forwards picking up full-backs instead of it being the other way around.

The style of play often worked for us. At home in games against Celtic, for example, the counter-attacking technique we had perfected operated to our advantage. They used to hurl themselves forward into attack after attack and we simply soaked up the pressure and then hit them on the break. It brought us a lot of important results against them. And we held our own with Aberdeen too in games which were almost always a battle of wits between Jim McLean and Alex Ferguson. They were interesting games to play in and there was rarely much between us over these seaons.

Rangers were the one club, though, who were always a stumbling block for us. No matter how well we were playing and how poorly Rangers were doing – and around then they were not a particularly potent force – we found it hard against them. It was always a problem trying to get a result at Ibrox and even at Tannadice they could surprise us. It was unbelievable.

It was in Europe, though, that the tactics the manager had devised for us paid off most of all. Dropping into defence away from home, just as we did every other week in the Premier League, was not a problem for us at all. It was the kind of game we were accustomed to playing. We suffered none of the problems that other Scottish teams encountered going abroad in the various tournaments. It was something we had been trained to do. It had been drilled into us and so when we had to play away from home against top flight European opposition it was something we found comfortable rather than a way of playing the game which was unusual for us.

While I found fault with playing that way in some of the games in Scotland when, if we had been more positive, we would have been winning more often away from home, I have to admit that for the UEFA Cup and the European Cup the tactics were just right. Often we found ourselves playing the Continentals at what had always been considered their game – and coming out on top.

There were some famous results before I made it into the team and some just as famous after I had made my European breakthrough. And, season after season, United used to be the team left carrying the flag for Scotland while the more famous clubs, like the Old Firm, were out in the early rounds. Those were exciting times and they were good times to learn about the game. It's only by playing in Europe on a fairly regular basis that you can get to grips with the differences in approach adopted by opposing teams from various countries. The experience I collected in four years in Europe with United returned to help a lot last season when Rangers reached the European Champions' League for the first time. That run by Rangers reminded me of the lengthy forays into Europe that we enjoyed at Tannadice so often.

My first involvement in Europe came in one of the matches United fans still remember fondly. It was in the UEFA Cup against the French side Monaco. We went to the tiny principality and beat them 5-2 on their own ground, won the Tannadice return 2-1 and were through on aggregate. In the second round we went in against Borussia Moenchengladbach – and this time while we lost 2-0 on their ground we scored another five goals in the Tannadice clash and were through again. Another five-goal romp saw us through against Winterslag of Belgium who had defeated Arsenal in the previous round.

Suddenly we found ourselves in the quarter-finals where we were drawn against a Yugoslav side, Radnicki Nis. Like ourselves Radnicki were not a household name feared across Europe but their record that season was formidable. They had knocked out Napoli and Grasshoppers of Zurich in the opening rounds – each time on the away goals' ruling. Then they had defeated the Dutch cracks Feyenoord, so while it was a journey into the unknown for us their season's results spoke for themselves. Maybe the defeat of Grasshoppers was not particularly impressive – but their ability to beat any Italian team and then a side with the reputation and resources of Feyenoord told us that we faced a troublesome tie.

What we were not prepared for, however, was how the cards were stacked against us when we made the long journey for the second leg of that quarter-final. In the opening match we had won 2-0 at Tannadice and we felt that with the confidence we had been building up in Europe we could handle anything they cared to throw at us. I still believe we could have done if one of the main problems had not been a referee who came from just across the border in Bulgaria and who was fêted as a local hero before and after the match. He certainly deserved his hero's welcome afterwards – he had earned that with his decisions during the game.

It's hard enough going to a place in the Yugoslav provinces without also having to contend with a local referee – and that's what he was. Yes, he was Bulgarian but from a town just 40 or so miles away from where he was playing. He did us no favours, especially in a second half where they scored the three goals which put us out. When that second half came around we had been intimidated by the refereeing. We were penalised for the slightest signs of a physical challenge. The Bulgarian official gave foul after foul against us. Almost every tackle we made brought the whistle, and that put us under pressure from a succession of free kicks which would not have been given under normal circumstances.

It got to the stage where we were reluctant to make proper challenges and this allowed them the freedom to attack us while we could put up only token resistance. They scored twice. The opening goal arrived eight minutes after half time and the crucial second – that levelled the score on aggregate – came 17 minutes from the end. Then in 83 minutes the moment we had all been fearing arrived – the referee gave them a penalty. It was a decision well in keeping with all the others he had given – but it remains in my memory as one of the craziest ever given against any team I have been playing for. Hamish McAlpine had come off his line to punch away a cross. He connected, the ball went clear and as he came down he collided with a Yugoslav forward who was racing into the penalty box. Down went the attacker, over ran the ref blowing his whistle and pointing to the spot. It was just what we had feared, just what we had expected, but the way it came still made it hard to accept. They scored and then went on to lose heavily to Hamburg in the semi-finals. We were so disappointed at the result but, again, it was part of the learning process.

Things like that should not happen. But they do and you have to adjust to them, you have to be able to accept that the treatment you receive away from home is not going to resemble in the slightest the treatment you should get. Whether that comes from referees – as it was that day in Yugoslavia – or from opposition players or supporters it is something you simply have to live with. On occasions it is not easy to do that but the more games you play in European tournaments then the more you realise what can go on and the more you learn that the one way of beating any of the dirty tricks campaigns you have to face up to is by playing your best football and winning by skill and ability. You also have to try to make sure that the opposition get no idea at all that they may be upsetting you. Grit your teeth and get on with the job in hand is the best way of dealing with the problems. If they do think they are getting to you then they will step up whatever pressure they are bringing to bear on you in a bid to make you crack. Psychologically you have to be ready for all of that. Getting an early lesson was good for me, I think. Certainly I've never had to face refereeing as bad or as biased as that since! But when I have felt that things are not going in our direction I'm able to adapt my game and be more wary when going into tackles, making sure that a referee isn't given the slightest chance of penalising challenges made in or around the penalty box. It isn't easy but it's something that sometimes has to be done.

The following season we were back in the UEFA Cup tournament and, once again, we reached the last eight while other bigger, better known British clubs crashed out in the early rounds. All four of the representatives from England, Arsenal, Manchester United, Ipswich and Southampton, were beaten in the first-round. Rangers got to round two and then lost 6-2 on aggregate to the German Bundesliga side Cologne.

While that massacre of British hopes was taking place we made steady progress in the same way the club had been doing over the years. Our first-round opponents were the wealthy and powerful Dutch team PSV Eindhoven. We drew 1-1 at home and were more or less written off until we went to Holland, adopted the counter-attacking style we used so effectively away from home and beat them 2-0. It was an extraordinary result and it came because of the experience the lads had gathered over the previous seasons and the patience the manager had demanded that we show. In the second round it was something of a repeat when we beat the Norwegians Viking Stavanger 3-1 over there and then could only draw 0-0 at Tannadice. Our away form was carrying us through and it was almost as impressive in our next tie when we had to meet the German side Werder Bremen. The hammering Rangers had received was a warning to us. Indeed it looked even more ominous when we beat Werder Bremen 2-1 at home – the same result Rangers had managed at Ibrox against Cologne. Then they had lost five goals in an astonishing collapse in the away game. We didn't. Instead we found that playing the Continentals at their own game, at that cat-and-mouse game they enjoy so much, paid off once more. We drew 1-1 in Bremen and were in the last eight alongside some of the Continent's top clubs. Roma and Benfica and Valencia and Anderlecht were there and we wanted to pit ourselves against one of them. But, as happened so often with United, we were drawn to go behind the Iron Curtain – one of those trips into Eastern Europe which no player enjoyed. We were paired with the Czech side, Bohemians Prague whose only result of note in that season's competition had been putting out St Etienne, We had hopes of a semi-final spot – but it was not to be. The team we were tipped to beat scored the only goal of the two-legged tie on their own ground and it was enough to see us off.

It was a disappointment – but eventually we were to see it as something of a blessing in disguise because we were allowed to forget about the European challenge and concentrate on winning the Premier League title. It was a prize the club had never won before and one which had always seemed out of reach of the basically home-spun Tannadice team. This time, though, it was within our grasp and while a European semi-final would have been a marvellous lift for the club the championship was always going to be the priority.

If we had had to play on two fronts – at home and in Europe – then we might have slipped up. As it was the title was not settled until the last day of the season and even then it was a sweat for us. We had to go across the street to Dens Park to play our local rivals Dundee in a 'derby' game and we knew we had to win the game to be champions. Celtic, our closest rivals, had to go to Ibrox to face Rangers – a tough prospect at any time for them.

Anyhow, we were 2-1 up against Dundee and playing well, without any of the signs of nerves you might have expected us to have under the circumstances. At half time wee Jim told us that Rangers were up 2-0 so it looked as if we could even lose the lead we had and still take the flag. Luckily, though, we held on and at the end we found out that Celtic had won 4-2. If we had allowed our concentration to slip then we could conceivably have lost the game and the title. That would have been disastrous for all of us. But we celebrated on our rivals' ground, just as the other players had done when they won the two League Cup tournaments, and looked forward to our European Champions' Cup debut the following season.

Here we were, the 'corner shop club', as we had been dubbed, in against the giants, the very cream of European football. The UEFA Cup was a strong competition. Teams who took part in that were there usually because they had been second or third in their national league. That meant their form had been consistent over the previous season, unlike the entrants for the European Cup Winners' Cup where a team could qualify as beaten finalists and may have reached the final after a series of lucky one-off results.

But the Champions' Cup was the pinnacle for club football in Europe. When we went into the draw that summer of 1983 we went in alongside some of the most legendary names in the game – Ajax from Holland, Standard Liege from Belgium, Benfica from Portugal, the holders Hamburg from West Germany, Roma from Italy, Rapid Vienna from Austria and the English champions Liverpool.

It was a mouth-watering prospect for our supporters and an exciting challenge for all of us as players. So, when the draw was made for the first-round games at the ceremony in Switzerland it was a bit of a let down when we found ourselves drawn against Hamrun Spartans of Malta. The fans' dreams of visiting one of the great soccer capitals of the Continent had to be placed on hold. As far as we were concerned, sure it was a bit of a come-down from our expectations – but as professionals we knew that it is often best to feel your way into a European competition with an easy draw in the first round. We played in a double-header that day on the George Cross Island with Rangers, who were in the Cup Winners' Cup, facing Valetta in the first game that afternoon. They won 8-0 – setting us a target which we never looked like reaching. We were happy enough to coast to a comfortable 3-0 victory, a result which we repeated in the return in Dundee two weeks later.

Now we found ourselves in with the big guns. The cannon fodder had gone and, in the main, the clubs who were left were those with a European pedigree. We drew one of them – Standard Liege. The Belgians had been hit a season or two earlier by a bribes scandal but they had rebuilt their team. They had a smattering of international players from Belgium as well as two attacking imports. Simon Tahamata had come from Ajax while the powerful Horst Hrubesch, a West German international striker, had also joined them. On paper they looked formidable opponents, the kind we had expected to find in the tournament.

Yet in the first leg away from home, we played superbly well. In the Stade Slessin where Standard had an impressive European record we held them to a 0-0 draw. We did survive a goal-line clearance when Paul Hegarty stopped a shot which had beaten Hamish McAlpine just before half time. But we also went close ourselves with a Ralph Milne shot which struck the bar. Even that hardest of taskmasters, Jim McLean, declared that he was pleased with the performance. And he must have been even happier in the second leg when we hammered in four goals to add another famous result to those which had gone before. I believe that result made other clubs still in the tournament sit up and take notice of the near-unknown team from Scotland. The reputation we had been able to carve out for ourselves in the UEFA Cup was one thing – but in the Champions' Cup we were still new boys alongside so many of the others. We were in there matching ourselves against teams which had cost millions of pounds

The determination and will to win that Jim McLean recognised so early
in Richard Gough is etched on his features in this portrait
(Evening Times)

*Happy days with Jim McLean were not to last – Richard Gough and
other players hoist the Dundee United manager shoulder-high after
winning the Premier League title. Ibrox coach Davie Dodds is second
from the right (© D. C. Thomson & Co. Ltd)*

*Richard Gough with goalkeeper Hamish McAlpine, the man the
Rangers skipper believes would have revelled in the new pass back rule
(© D. C. Thomson & Co. Ltd)*

Following in father's footsteps? You never know, as young Michael learns about heading the ball from his dad! (Evening Times)

Rangers v Dunfermline: Champions again – Rangers manager Graeme Souness holds aloft the League Trophy as Mark Walters, Richard Gough and Davie Dodds look on, April 1990 (Evening Times)

The aerial power which impressed Walter Smith as Gough was growing up as a young player at Tannadice is displayed in a clash with Motherwell (Evening Times)

Gough makes a despairing tackle against Steaua in the European Cup quarter-final clash with the Romanians (Evening Times)

Richard Gough rises above his former team-mate Gary Mabbutt in this clash at Ibrox with his old side Spurs. Terry Butcher and Mo Johnston are the other Rangers players in the picture (Evening Times)

Even the fittest of players can suffer injury. Here Gough lies in agony after taking a knock in a clash with Hibs (Evening Times)

Happier times for Terry Butcher seen here celebrating his last triumph as Rangers captain – the Premier League title in 1990. A few months later his career was to end in tears and he was transferred. Richard Gough is extreme left in the back row (Evening Times)

The power and strength and determination which makes Gough Walter Smith's automatic choice as Rangers captain (Evening Times)

The Scottish Cup jinx is over and Rangers have beaten Airdrie in the final. Walter Smith joins the players in their celebrations. Gough believes Smith is 'closer' to the players than Graeme Souness was during his reign (Evening Times)

Richard Gough came back to Rangers for several reasons – one of them was Walter Smith, the perfect foil for Graeme Souness as the Rangers revolution took place (Evening Times)

A trophy win as the Rangers skipper holds the Scottish Cup aloft Andy Goram looks on (Evening Times)

to put together. Our team, apart from Paul Hegarty, who cost next to nothing to sign, and Eamonn Bannon, who cost around £150,000, was a home-grown one. That in itself helped make us almost unique in the high-powered atmosphere of Europe's number one tournament. Mind you, it didn't give us any kind of inferiority complex. We felt we could match the best.

Ralph Milne scored two of our goals against Standard that night while Paul Hegarty and Davie Dodds grabbed one each. That result carried us into the quarter-finals of the tournament – with the next tie being played in March. We now had a winter's break from Europe but thinking about what lay ahead still dominated our thoughts.

When the draw was made we found ourselves facing Rapid Vienna, the Austrian champions who had that country's top player, striker Hans Krankl, as their main threat with backing from midfielder Anton Panenka who was one of the great Czech stars of that time. On their way into the last eight they had knocked out the French champions Nantes and then our old rivals Bohemians of Prague in the second round. Impressive – but with our growing confidence in handling these European matches it was not a team we felt we could not defeat over the two matches.

Straight away we were happy that we had been drawn to play away from home first. That suited us. I think most teams prefer to play the first leg of any tie in a European tournament on the opposition ground. Then you can return home knowing exactly what has to be done – and knowing that you will be doing it on your pitch in front of your own fans. Derek Stark gave us the lead with a long-range shot – a spectacular goal it was too – and also a vital away goal which would prove even more important before the tie was over. They scored twice after that opener from us and we had to hang on grimly – but we knew that one goal, just a single goal at Tannadice would be enough to take us through to the last four. In the return Davie Dodds scored that goal and while we had some nervous moments we won the match 1-0 – the away goal we had grabbed in Vienna was enough to give us the result we wanted. And now there were only four . . . ourselves, Liverpool, Roma and Dinamo Bucharest.

The Romanians were, perhaps, the weakest opponents we could hope for. Yet they had beaten the holders Hamburg – and done so decisively with a 3-0 win in Bucharest and then a narrow 3-2 defeat in the Volksparkstadion in Hamburg. Impressive! Roma were the Italian champions, which is always recommendation enough. Liverpool, well, they were Liverpool. The Liverpool of Dalglish, Souness and Hansen who had been so powerful in European tournaments over the years. Balancing the belief that Dinamo Bucharest would be the easiest of the three clubs, though, was the prospect of going behind the Iron Curtain with all the attendant problems of poor food, miserable surroundings and a long flight.

When we were paired with Roma there were no complaints from the lads. I think we all knew that when people stressed that there were few easy touches in the Continent's number one tournament that was more or less right. When you got down to the last four then it was undoubtedly correct. We had to get on with it and the fact that so few clubs had reached this stage before us helped lift our feelings.

Since the European Cup had kicked off back in 1956 only four other Scottish teams had gone as far as we had. Celtic, of course, had won the tournament in 1967 and reached another final in 1970 as well as two other semi-final appearances in 1972 and 1974. Rangers had been in a semi-final in 1960, Dundee in 1963 and back in the inaugural competition Hibs had gone to the last four. It was an élite band of Scottish clubs we had joined and it was a good feeling to be among them. I think we all recognised that our achievement had been considerable. And we wanted to savour every moment of the two matches which now lay ahead.

Unhappily, as well as defeat, trouble loomed for us in one of the ugliest European ties in which I have ever been involved. The worry which nagged at me as the matches approached was that Roma knew the final was to be played on their home ground, Rome's Olympic Stadium. That had already been announced by UEFA and so the Italians were well aware of the fact that if they could knock us out of the tournament then they could win the trophy after a single game on their home pitch in front of their huge army of fans. It was a massive incentive for their players. After all, how often do teams get the opportunity of winning a European trophy on their own pitch?

This time we were playing the first match at Tannadice and we did win. We went out to play the game as a British-style cup-tie and that unsettled them. Derek Stark and Davie Dodds scored for us and we won 2-0, but I have to admit that I thought we were a little bit fortunate to get that result. They played well at Tannadice. They hit the bar and they didn't have the best of luck with their finishing but we had achieved the result we wanted and we had stopped them getting an away goal. We were happy – and then the trouble began!

For whatever reason their President came out with an astonishing attack on us. He accused us of being on drugs. He insisted that we had to have taken stimulants to be able to perform at such a high level for 90 minutes. The Italian Press fastened on to the claims and suddenly we, as players, found ourselves at the centre of this storm.

The fact that it was absolutely untrue did not seem to matter. In fact I remember Jim McLean joking about the allegations in our own newspapers. To some extent we did not take all of this seriously. It was hard to believe that another team would stoop to these off-field smears.

I still don't know why it happened but I do believe that there might have been a combination of circumstances at work. Number one, the Roma President who had spent millions of pounds to assemble his side was probably angry, embarrassed and upset that they could not overcome a small club like Dundee United. Number two, Roma knew that if they failed to get to the final then their fans, looking forward to seeing them in that final, would feel humiliated. The pressure on them was greater than normal – but it would never have occurred to a British team to come out with these allegations. Italian football, where the prizes are greater and the expectations enormous, is different. Anything goes at times and on this particular occasion the victims were going to be us.

It was clear that we were heading into a very hostile situation when we travelled to Rome for the second leg. No matter what the club said, the Italian fans were convinced by now that we were the villains of the piece. The club asked SFA secretary Ernie Walker and the Scotland manager Jock Stein to accompany the official party which flew to Italy. I think they wanted to have neutrals with some standing and authority to be there in case the trouble worsened.

It did get worse just as we all expected. If we had thought the problems were bad when we played Radnicki Nis a couple of seasons earlier then that seemed like a picnic compared to the reception we received in Rome. On the way to the game bricks were hurled at the team bus. When we got there the atmosphere was really threatening. Some remark which Jim McLean was supposed to have made had brought headlines in the Italian newspapers and further incensed the supporters. They made things hot for us and yet they had the talent in their team to make all of that unnecessary.

They had the Brazilian midfielder Cerezo and they had two players who had been in the Italian World Cup-winning side in Spain just a couple of years earlier. Conti was one and Graziani was the other and they had other good players – the playmaker Di Bartolemi and the man who was the striking partner for Graziani up front, Pruzzo. They were outstanding players and they had shown their skills at Tannadice. But somewhere in that club there was an element which wanted to cause us the maximum of aggravation, an element which was not content to rely on the skills of their players but hoped that the pressures from the crowd would get to us . . .

It was that element which certainly helped Roma reach the final at our expense. Ralph Milne missed an early chance for us and from then on we rarely matched the Italian champions. To some extent the team crumbled in that hate-filled Olympic Stadium. Pruzzo scored twice and Di Bartolemi got the vital third goal with a penalty. We were out.

At the end some of the Italian players raced towards our dugout and Jim McLean was threatened by them. The goalkeeper Tancredi spat abuse at the manager as he tried to get back to the safety of the dressing-room. It was dreadful and it made us wonder what might have happened if we had held on to our lead and stopped Roma getting to the final!

I have looked back to that game many times since, wondering if there was anything we could have done to change things. Trying to think of something different we could have tried to alter the course of the game. But I don't think there was any way we could have prevented the trouble and the abuse and the threats from the Rome fans which affected us. And, even if Ralphe Milne had scored then I'm sure they would have still done enough to go through.

It was almost as if their appearance in the final before their adoring support had been pre-ordained – and there was no way a team of unknowns from Scotland would have been allowed to wreck that dream. Later it was discovered that the club President had tried to make sure of victory against us by attempting to bribe the referee. The man in charge was a Frenchman, and a good, top-class referee, Joel Quiniou. Whatever happened, the money – and it was alleged to have been around £50,000 – never reached him. And he handled the game well. I still remember how he disallowed a goal from Bruno Conti when one of his linesmen signalled that another player had strayed into an offside position. I was convinced that it was a good goal but he chalked it off and the President must have been wondering what had happened to all his cash. Apparently it went missing and the referee emerged with his reputation untainted – but the President was forced to resign. If all that had been discovered earlier then, perhaps, we would have been in the final and Roma might have been disqualified. But it was much later before the scandal surfaced. By then Roma had received their just deserts. They lost on penalties to Liverpool in the final.

They were a shadow of the team which had played us that night they faced the Anfield team. Beforehand I would have backed them to win that one. They had their fans there. They were at home. And the European Cup was within their grasp. Yet they were strangely negative. It was as if they were afraid of Liverpool's reputation. And I reckon that they over-estimated Liverpool just as much as they had under-estimated us before they arrived at Tannadice. If they had shown the same aggression against the English champs as they had against us then they would have won. I'm still sure of that.

But the game we saw on television that night had no passion. It was like a game of chess. Phil Neal put Liverpool in front and then Graziani equalised and Roma sat back. Instead of going for victory they were cautious and careful and the match ran into extra time and then a penalty shoot-out which they lost. I'm certain that they handed Liverpool too much respect. I could have understood that if they had been playing the final on a neutral ground. At home it was a mistake and they paid for it, I'm happy to say. Our second-leg clash with them in Rome remains one of those days that few of the players particularly want to remember!

The next season we were back in the UEFA Cup and reached the third round before going out in a Battle of Britain clash with Manchester United. It was another disappointment but it was another game which raised the status of the club. If we had been able to impress Europe in previous seasons – now we were able to impress the English.

We did that by drawing 2-2 at Old Trafford and then losing out in a 3-2 defeat at Tannadice in the second leg. We did well and years afterwards their then manager, Ron Atkinson, was still talking about how well Billy Kirkwood, now on the backroom staff at Ibrox, had marked Bryan Robson. Hamish had another wonder night at Old Trafford and even though they had a multi-talented team we should have been able to win at home. It was another disappoint-ment – but we had shown that we could match one of the world's biggest clubs and the United players were quick to say how hard we had pushed them over the two games. It goes down as another honourable defeat and the Manchester United pennant joined the other battle honours in the Tannadice boardroom.

There are a few there now. Some marking disappointments certainly, but many more saluting famous victories. I'm happy that I played a part in some of them. Happy, too, that Jim McLean spotted qualities in me as a young player which persuaded him to offer me a contract. That has been his greatest talent – being able to unearth young players and mould them for a future career.

Where he fails is in handling players who have strong views of their own – I was one of them – and, also, in being over-cautious when sometimes a bolder approach might have brought him still more success, including a Scottish Cup win he has never been able to savour.

I'm sorry my last days were troubled ones but the feud since then has been one way. And wee Jim must know that.

CHAPTER FIVE

Flops in Europe

One of the major disappointments I had when I first arrived at Ibrox was the way we seemed to flop in Europe. We had a team with tremendous potential but for one reason or another in those first few seasons at the club I found that we were knocked out of competitions in the early rounds. It was a stark contrast to the days at Tannadice when we were guaranteed to be marching on in Europe after the winter break almost every season. And these disappointments hammered home to me the very fine line which exists between success and failure in the top tournaments.

Split seconds can decide games. One mistake can mean the difference between victory and defeat and, always, the cruel glare of publicity highlights those moments. One of the attractions of returning to Rangers was the regular involvement in European football that it offered. The fact that it was so brief, until that run which took us to the verge of the European Cup final last season, was something which gnawed at me continually.

It was also a fact which was hurled at us by supporters of other clubs and it gave further ammunition to the critics from down south who saw Rangers being able to win what they termed a 'Mickey Mouse' league but unable to make any kind of mark in Europe. At this time English clubs were still banned following the Heysel disaster and so our games became a focus for Fleet Street writers as well as the Scottish-based writers. We certainly provided them with ammunition enough to criticise us over a few seasons. And yet it was not always the case that we flopped or that we let ourselves down when it came to these big games. Sometimes we simply came up against class acts very early on.

That first year back was a troubled one for the club because of injuries and at one stage a poor run of results and other on- and off-field problems. Almost immediately I returned we won the Skol Cup and it was one of the few highlights I could share with the lads. Earlier they had knocked out Dyamo Kiev in the first round of the European Cup and then went on to defeat the Polish champions Gornik. I had arrived at the time of the Gornik tie which was played in October and November but was not eligible. So the 4-2 aggregate victory meant that I would be playing in the Champions' Cup when it resumed in March. At the start of the year we learned that we would have to trek behind the Iron Curtain yet again – the third time for most of the lads in that one season. We were drawn against Steaua Bucharest who had won the competition two years earlier by defeating Barcelona on penalties in Seville. They still had most of the players who had shocked the Spanish giants that night in 1986 – and had added a new star in the wonder boy of Romanian football, Gheorgi Hagi. We knew it would be difficult – and yet I felt confident that I would be playing in a European Cup semi-final once again. We had avoided the West German champions Bayern Munich, the great Real Madrid, Benfica from Portugal and the Dutch cracks PSV Eindhoven in the last eight. Alongside them Steaua looked a shade easier opposition even though the travel and the surroundings would be as difficult as always. Personally, I thought that was a small price to pay if we were to have the opportunity of getting into the last four.

Things, however, did not go as I had hoped and anticipated just as is the way of things in Europe. We went into the game as favourites but the bookies had not told the Romanians that and we crashed to defeat in the first leg.

It's a cardinal rule in these games away from home that you try to frustrate the opposition as much as possible in the early stages of the game. The theory is that once you do that then their fans will turn against the team and the players will drop the level of their performances. Sometimes it works, other times it doesn't. But, in the main, it is a tactical approach which almost everyone adopts against experienced opponents away from home. Our hopes of achieving any kind of frustration disappeared after a couple of minutes. That's how long it took them to score on a pitch which was a mud heap because of torrential rain. When they scored again 25 minutes from the end of the game we knew that the return was going to be difficult.

In the first round the lads had lost just 1-0 to Dinamo Kiev – a penalty goal which was scored by Alexei Mikhailichenko, now a Rangers player. That set them up for a 2-0 win at home and in the second round they had beaten Gornik 3-1 at Ibrox and then drawn 1-1 in Katowice. So we had not been in a situation where we had to score three goals to clinch victory – and we guessed that life was not going to be easy for us at Ibrox.

When we were caught cold and lost another early goal – Lacatus scored it – it was over. We fought back. I scored after quarter of an hour and Ally McCoist got a second with a penalty after 30 minutes – but the damage had been done. They knew we needed two more goals and they

73

closed ranks and made sure that we were not going to get them. They were a good side and Hagi was a magnificent player but I still feel today that they were a team we could have beaten. Benfica saw them off in the semi-final with a 2-0 win in Lisbon being enough to take them into the final against PSV Eindhoven.

The following season I was back on familiar territory – in the UEFA Cup where Dundee United had carved out their European reputation. But, once again, we were out before the competition was properly under way. We kicked off with another Iron Curtain trek to Katowice in Poland where we played the team of that name. At Ibrox we won by the only goal of the game – over there we won 4-2 with a performance which had me believing that we would be able to reach the later stages of the competition. In round two we met the West Germans Cologne and in the Mungersdorf Stadium we held out at 0-0 until the closing minutes when we lost two goals and had Ally McCoist sent off. Two lapses of concentration saw us throw away all the disciplined work we had put in during the early parts of the match. It was a cruel blow – and at Ibrox two weeks later we failed again. This time we didn't get a goal until late – Kevin Drinkell got it – but then when we went looking for another we were caught at the back, they equalised and the tie was pushed beyond our reach.

Somehow or other for all the experience we had in the team we didn't seem to be absorbing the lessons of Europe. Neither Steaua nor Cologne were outstanding opponents but they had been too organised for us in the two-leg ties. Man for man we were probably better than either of them – but we were left licking our wounds as they continued in European tournament play. For the second time in less than a year I found myself wondering where things had gone wrong and vowing that we would put them right the next time round. The trouble was that we didn't – but this time, at least, we were facing top opposition which made defeat slightly easier to accept. Bayern were old European foes of Rangers and while some of their greatest names had gone they had unearthed new heroes and new stars.

Olaf Thom was there and so was Klaus Augenthaler. The former Celtic player Alan McInally was also with the West German champions. I missed the first game, which was at Ibrox, because of injury. But even if I'd been fit I doubt if I could have done enough to influence the result. We lost 3-1 with just a goal from Mark Walters to cheer the 40,000 fans who had come to see us notch a famous European victory. I can still recall a stunning goal from Augenthaler, now one of the Bayern coaches, leaving poor Chris Woods helpless. It was a spectacular long-range drive and it was a sickener for the lads. We drew in Munich – a drab 0-0 result – and, really, all we had gone there to do was salvage some of the self-respect which we had lost at Ibrox. We performed well enough but we did so against a side which knew they had only to go through the motions to be in the second round.

Bayern were at their peak then. They were formidable opponents and while it was a blow to go out so early we were reassured by the fact that we had lost this time to a superb outfit. They proved that as they progressed, winning home and away against PSV Eindhoven and only losing in the semi-final to AC Milan. Even though they only went out on the away goals' rule. There was no disgrace attached to that particular short foray into Europe . . .

Nor was there any shame in the way we went out the following year even though we found ourselves severely criticised at the time of the game. I don't think the critics realised just how good a team the Yugoslavs were . . . nor did we. We found out the hard way.

First of all we had had an easy passage from the first round with a tie against Valetta of Malta – we won 4-0 away from home, hammered in another six at Ibrox and felt we had eased ourselves into the tournament rather well. Then the roof caved in when we went to Belgrade for our first match against Red Star. We lost 3-0 and the tie was over before we took them back to Ibrox. Our fans knew it, too.

Red Star arrived to find a half-empty stadium – we had attracted just 24,000 fans to the game – and they duly collected a 1-1 draw and went on their way to the next round. Indeed they went a bit further than that because they went all the way to the final before they beat Marseille in a penalty shoot-out in Italy . . .

Yet when they defeated us no one in Scotland seemed to see they had the potential to take the trophy. Instead we found ourselves hammered for losing to what was being termed a 'team of unknowns'! Yet it was a team which had Darko Pancev and Dejan Savicevic and Robert Prosinecki in their line-up. Eventually they were recognised as the finest team to come out of Yugoslavia in decades. It was just a pity for us that we had to come across them in the second round of the competition – and a pity, too, that so few of our critics could not see just how good a team they were.

I still reckon we could have been better informed on Red Star before that first game. I don't know if we would have been able to beat them – frankly I doubt it – but we might have been able to cope with their attacks just a little better. I can remember that after about ten minutes of the game their right-winger – I think his name was Binic – had hit our bye-line three times and got crosses into our box. He was a flying machine – but we had not been told that before the match. You know, we lost 3-0 and it might have been more. We didn't get a kick. By the time we had found out just how good their players were they were in command and they remained there. It was an embarrassing game for us, especially as we had hoped to make some kind of impression on Europe that year after the early exit at the hands of Bayern the previous season.

We had really known very little about them and there were occasions when I saw that as a flaw in the preparations we made for Europe when Graeme Souness was in charge. Very often Graeme went on the Liverpool theory that you didn't want to know too much about your opponents. It was better to go out and play every game the same way more or less. Just use the normal approach for any European tie and, in essence, let the opposition worry about what you might do to them. That attitude had been very successful for Liverpool over the years – their European Cup wins proved that. But their reputation went before them. Other clubs did worry about having to face them because of the European pedigree they had built up over the years. We had still to make any impact on the Continent and so when the Liverpool way was translated to our own situation it didn't work out quite as it should have done.

The next season brought another first round exit and no one was to blame for that one except ourselves . . . because this was a tie we had won and then we tossed it away. Once more it was an Iron Curtain team we played – we were getting quite used to Eastern Europe by now – and while Sparta Prague were organised and competent they were anything but convincing against us.

All I can say is that they were a competent side with several good quality players, including Jiri Nemec who scored their goal in the first leg in Czechoslovakia. Their captain and midfielder Vaclav Nemecek was another highly skilled international but we were the better team over the two games. At Ibrox more than 34,000 fans saw one of our new signings, Stuart McCall, get a goal to put us level. We tried for another breakthrough but they defended intelligently and the match moved into extra time. Again Stuart McCall scored and victory was there until a blunder between Scott Nisbet and Andy Goram saw Nissy score an own goal. I was out injured and watched in agony as another European dream turned to dust. It was a terrible goal to lose and we all knew that.

We were also conscious that this was Walter Smith's first European tie as a manager and we had let him down. As players we had to hold our hands up. It simply underlined how these ties can hinge on one mistake, one little lapse in concentration, one tiny misjudgment. It was some consolation – though not much – when Sparta knocked out Marseille in the second round and went into the first ever Champions' League set up. They finished second to Barcelona in their group, chased the Spanish champions all the way – and it was Barcelona who won the European Cup that season.

Yet the feeling remained that we should have done better and it nagged away at me for the rest of the season. I was beginning to wonder if we were ever going to be able to silence some of the jeers from rival supporters and, at the same time, give the club some prominence on the much larger European stage.

It was also about time that we gave our supporters the chance to celebrate some successes abroad. Yes, we had given them the title again by the end of that season. And we had ended our jinx run with victory in the Scottish Cup. But we wanted more . . . and they wanted more . . . and the next season we were able to give them a European campaign which matches any in the club's long, long history.

CHAPTER SIX

The Champions' League

We had had to watch from the sidelines, so to speak, when the European Champions' League kicked off in the 1991-92 season. It was galling for us because we knew that on any other night we would have beaten Sparta Prague and then, who knows, we might have been able to move into the new set up ourselves.

But it was galling for another reason. Because it was Rangers who had suggested the changes in the format for the European tournaments. The chairman, David Murray, had felt that Europe should be moving towards some kind of Super League and a blueprint for change had been drawn up and submitted to UEFA, the governing body of the game right across Europe. With some amendments that document had been accepted and the Champions' League was the first step towards a set up which would keep the major clubs happy.

There had been unease for some time when top teams, built for European competition, had gone out for whatever reasons in early rounds. Huge investment had been lost and the big guns wanted some kind of protection – not from the possibility of defeat, because that is always there, but from lost revenue. A league where guaranteed games provided guaranteed income was seen as the answer and already that has been so successful in the Champions' Cup that changes are envisaged for the other competitions also.

It was, of course, the Champions' Cup which concerned us, and we had seen how the top eight teams had coped with the league format the previous season, the Champions' League – the new set up began from the quarter-finals with the winners of each group of four meeting in a final on a neutral ground. Each team, though, knew from the start that they would get *three* home games and the revenue from these games.

It was an attractive innovation for the clubs and, in the second season, it was clear that it had also been a success with the major television companies and important sponsors. The pay-off for teams which reached this last eight stage could be as much as five million pounds. Money came from television rights and sponsorship simply for being in the élite groups of four. More money, from the same source, rewarded merit. Teams were given cash for every point they collected in their games. And, naturally, clubs kept their home gates. It was a bonanza – if we could throw off the jinx which had haunted us in the Continent's number one tournament. We felt that this time we simply had to succeed.

The club had given the rest of Europe the basis for the new-look tournament – it would seem strange if Rangers were not going to be able to take part in it!

The new players Walter Smith had added to the squad when he took over – bringing in as many Scots as he could to cover the foreigners' rule which had hit our club particularly hard – had settled in. Andy Goram, David Robertson and Stuart McCall had now become key players and Walter had bought Scotland defender Dave McPherson in the summer to strengthen the quality and depth of Scottish players in the first-team pool.

I looked at the squad and, given that so many of us now had international experience to add to our club back-grounds, I felt more confident that I had before any of the previous attempts we had made in our bid to find success in Europe.

All we needed, I thought, was a favourable draw to begin with building towards a slightly tougher second-round match, and with just a share of the breaks we could be in that glamorous group which would be recognised as the best in Europe. It was a tantalising thought as we awaited the first-round draw in July.

When it arrived we found ourselves against slightly better opposition that we might have found ideal. We didn't get anyone from Malta or Luxembourg or Cyprus or any of these smaller countries who, while they have improved in tactical awareness over the past few years, would not be expected to stop us heading towards our target. Instead of one of the rabbits we were drawn against the Danish champions Lyngby and my mind was catapulted back to the summer when the Danes had been crowned European Champions. And still further back to Mexico in 1986 when Scotland had faced the Danes in a World Cup match.

At one time clubs in Scotland were able to look on a trip to Scandinavia as more or less a walk-over in any of the European competitions. But these days were long gone. Swedish club teams had built up solid records in the Continental tournaments and the Danes, as European Champions, were on a high.

It was a situation which required caution and Walter Smith and Archie Knox treated Lyngby as they would have treated AC Milan. Both went to see them play. Their style of play was analysed, their weaknesses and strengths noted and their individual players examined in depth. Walter was convinced that the tie would be awkward and that only a performance of professionalism and complete concentration would take us through. As players we felt the same – but the warnings were important. They made sure that not a single player would go into the tie believing that Lyngby were anything other than quality opponents. Lyngby were a young side, but a side filled with confidence after their country's triumph in Sweden. We discovered that in the opening 20 minutes of the first-leg match at Ibrox. Forty thousands fans were in the stadium that night to see us kick off in another European Cup challenge and Lyngby gave all of them a nervous start. Not to mention the worries they gave us in the early stages of the game!

Twice in the first 20 minutes they could have gone in front. Twice they were through our defence and twice we survived to stop them getting an away goal and possibly puncturing any confidence we might have been feeling. Though the way they were playing then didn't do much to make us feel all that comfortable! Andy Goram had one great save and they were desperately close with another goal try. By this time we were feeling a little nervous and the crowd possibly sensed that. It took a goal from Mark Hateley just before half time to put us in control of the match. Even then, we lived dangerously on occasion before Pieter Huistra scored a second to give us a two-goal cushion to take with us to Copenhagen. We actually played better in the second leg and the way we approached the match heralded events to come. We were in command most of the time, we were disciplined and we played on the break, and it was from one of our counter attacks that Ian Durrant scored the only goal of that second-leg game. That was us through on a 3-0 aggregate and then we were plunged into the middle of a controversy which was none of our doing.

While we were going through, Leeds, the English champions, were going out in a dramatic clash against the German representatives Stuttgart. Somehow, though, the German coach had blundered by putting one too many foreign players in his squad for the game. It was an astonishing blunder especially coming from the Germans with their well-deserved reputation for efficiency. The 'foreign' players' ruling was something we knew all about, of course, because it had affected the English lads in our squad. Rangers had never taken the slightest chance and it was difficult to believe that no one had spotted the Stuttgart mistake until after the game . . . and, I mean 24 hours after the game. I'm sure if we had tried it on then it would have been noticed immediately. Now, though, we faced confusion over our next round opponents.

We were drawn to face one or other of the teams – but first they were forced into a play-off which had to take place in the Nou Camp Stadium in Barcelona. We were surprised at that order from UEFA. Most of us expected Stuttgart to be simply booted out of the tournament for breaking the rules. But the European bosses decided otherwise, a play-off was their answer and Barcelona was their venue. Justice was done when Leeds won and the stage was set for what the newspapers called the Battle of Britain!

It was a big, big challenge for us – but it was the game we wanted. From the time the draw was made and then the replay ordered we had talked about it in the dressing-room and every single player wanted to get the chance to meet the champions of England. Not that we thought we had anything to prove to them – but it was an opportunity to prove to a lot of media people in the south that we were something more than a big fish in a small pool. That was going to be important, to be able to wipe the sneers from some faces.

There is always extra rivalry in any Scotland v England confrontation and that was there. But even our English lads felt they had points to prove, particularly Mark Hateley, who had been overlooked by England boss Graham Taylor.

But I never felt that we needed to prove ourselves against them . . . we had proved ourselves time after time. We knew that their Premier League is stronger than our own in Scotland in the sense that there is quality throughout the league instead of just among the handful of leading clubs. Population alone would ensure that. But since the Graeme Souness-inspired revolution Rangers have been able to attract top English players and in cases like my own bring back top Scottish players from that league. As far as I was concerned that underlined just how *big* a club Rangers are. I think that the Leeds United players realised that too. Footballers do accept the status of the club.

I don't think the public always realise it and I know that the media people most certainly don't – they were the ones we had to win over. Yet before going into the two-leg clash I had made up my own mind on one thing – that no matter what happened Rangers were, and thankfully the general public know this now too, and will remain a *bigger* club than Leeds United.

More than 43,000 fans were at Ibrox even though the tie was restricted to our own fans with no visiting supporters from the south. The ticket scramble had been unbelievable and the noise when the teams went out that October night was incredible. I have never heard anything like the sound which greeted us and it was heartening to know that all of it was on our side. It was a passionate atmosphere and it brought a game to match the feelings of the fans. It was a British-type game, a cup-tie which was unlike any of the other ties we were to play in Europe that season.

While we may have been written off by the bulk of the public and Press down south we knew that the Leeds players would not take that attitude. They had Gordon Strachan and Gary McAllister to tell them how it would be at Ibrox and, in any case, there is a mutual respect among professionals. They knew we had a battery of international players to line up against them – just as we realised they had the same to throw in against us. Apart from their Scots they had Tony Dorigo and David Batty who were in the England side, Gary Speed from Wales and their French striker Eric Cantona. They had pipped Manchester United for the title the previous season and under their manager Howard Wilkinson had been moulded into one of the most feared and organised teams in England. Their home record was amazing and so we knew that we had to take some kind of advantage south with us when we travelled to Leeds for the second leg.

In less than a minute, though, these pre-match plans were put on hold and the stadium and that huge, fanatical crowd had been silenced. It was an unreal moment, one of those instants which will stay with me forever. The cauldron of noise was suddenly hushed as my Scotland team-mate Gary McAllister rifled in a long-range shot which beat Andy Goram – and which would have beaten any 'keeper – and ended in our net.

It was the worst possible start, the worst kind of opening you can suffer in any European tie. In this one it seemed so much worse because of what was at stake for the club. We had a larger view of the clash than just that Battle of Britain tag because we knew that we had flopped too often in Europe and that this season was the one where we had to try to put things right. To go out in the second round again was unthinkable. To go out to Leeds was now going to compound our embarrassment.

We had to battle back and the crowd, struck dumb in that opening minute, had to find their voices again. Both things happened in a game which pulsated with drama. It's on nights like that one – and also in the return at Elland Road – you realise just how potent British football can be. This was no normal cat-and-mouse European game – it was a red-blooded cup-tie with two teams trying to win the games. At the end of the 90 minutes we had won 2-1. Indeed, before half time we had gone in front with a fightback which had the whole of Ibrox behind the side once more. It was ironic that we were helped to victory by a blunder from the Leeds goalkeeper John Lukic after all the years that Scottish 'keepers were the butt of so many English jokes. He punched a corner from Ian Durrant into his own net and then Ally McCoist pushed us ahead. While we had conceded that away goal we were in control of the tie, though Leeds' fans remained convinced that their team had done enough to qualify for the Champions' League.

In other circumstances, the normal circumstances surrounding a European tie, they might have been right in thinking that way. But, as I've stressed, this was something else. This was different and even though we would not have any supporters with us for the second leg we knew that we could handle the atmosphere at Elland Road and we knew, too, that in an all-British context we could match Leeds. It was not the same as defending a single goal lead in Eastern Europe or in Italy or Spain or Germany. This was on our doorstep and we faced a team we knew inside out. They were not going to surprise us and tactically we knew exactly what we could expect from them.

In fact, after that first leg I said to the lads in the dressing-room I wondered how they would react if we hit them with an early goal just as they had hit us with one at Ibrox. I felt that we had shown an astonishing resilience and courage in the way we had battled back to win the game. Not every team would have been able to survive an early blow like that Gary McAllister goal. I didn't know how Leeds would react but it was something I hoped we could maybe find out. Never for a moment did I think that would be the scenario – but two weeks later it turned out that way. And the English champions didn't handle it nearly as well as we had!

In the opening minute Andy Goram – who was one of our heroes that night – made a superb save from Eric Cantona and almost immediately after that Mark Hateley scored as spectacular a goal as Gary had collected at Ibrox. The contrast in fortunes inside that minute clinched the tie for us. We had cancelled out the away goal they had scored at Ibrox and Andy had shown them what he was made of with that glorious save. It made me think again of the thin line between success and failure in Europe. If Cantona scores then they are in command, but it didn't happen that way . . .

Instead we had pushed ourselves two goals ahead and now Leeds had to score three goals to beat us. With the confidence the strike from Mark sent surging through the team there was little likelihood of that happening. We defended well. The goal allowed us to sit back and use a counter-attacking game which had suited us in Copenhagen and which again saw us playing within ourselves against Leeds. When Mark and Ally McCoist combined to get a second for us in the second half the tie was over. We knew it. Leeds knew it. And their supporters knew it. That second goal was another great piece of play from Mark who went clear of the Leeds defence and then struck a ball across goal for Ally to finish it off.

Near the end Cantona pulled one back for them but by now they recognised that they were playing for pride only. We had done enough to win and we deserved to win over the two games. They threw the lot at us that night in Leeds and we did more than simply survive, we won the game as well as the tie. Until that night they had gone 33 games at home without defeat. They had destroyed Stuttgart there in the second leg of the tie which was eventually declared invalid and at the time they played us, as well as being the reigning champions, they were also in third spot in the Premier League. The defeat from us killed them. It ended their season. Somehow or other they just collapsed after that tie.

It left me wondering what might have happened to us if the result had gone the other way. You just never know these things. I would like to think that we would have gone on to have just as successful a domestic season as we did have. But that game was such an important one. It was also a highly charged emotional occasion which left all of us drained . . . but when you win you shake off any feelings of strain or tiredness. It's when you lose all of that hits you. Just as it hit the Leeds players.

I have no doubts that our double victory over them killed them off as far as the rest of the season was concerned. They flopped in the cup competition and they slumped in the league and, if you asked any of their players, then I'm certain they would agree with me. The consequences of the defeat were severe.

For the players there was wounded pride and professionalism because huge television audiences had guaranteed vast interest in the clash. No one likes to fail when the entire country is looking on . . .

For the club there was the blow of not reaching the money-laden Champions' League. Millions of pounds were there to be earned and now the money was to flow into the Ibrox coffers rather than go to Leeds. I think, too, after winning against Stuttgart in Barcelona they perhaps thought they were destined to go on to great things in the competition. It was not to be and the disappointment hit them hard.

For us the games continued – and in an exciting new way. Two groups of four teams each were drawn and we found ourselves in with the tourney's number one seeds, Marseille of France, with the Belgian champions Bruges and the Russians of CSKA Moscow who had defeated the Cup holders Barcelona on their way to this part of the European Cup. In the other group were the favourites AC Milan, IFK Gothenburg from Sweden, Porto from Portugal and PSV Eindhoven from Holland.

The feelings in the dressing-room were mixed. We were happy to dodge Milan but we knew Marseille and we had already lost to them in a pre-season friendly at Ibrox! CSKA were unknown – but they had beaten Barcelona while Bruges, we knew, would be solid and dangerous like most Belgian sides. There was little to choose between the two groups – just as it had always been at this stage of the European Cup, the last eight rarely provide easy touches.

We had our first game at home – but to counter any advantage we felt from that the opposition was Marseille and we had suffered at their hands before the season began. We knew them as a multi-talented side. Experienced. Skilled. Organised. And tough!

What we didn't know is just how tough they would be. On that night at Ibrox they were the most physical side we were asked to face all season. It was unbelievable. They took us by surprise because that kind of physical approach was not what you expect from a French side. Or, indeed, from any European side. In fact they were not just hard. They were downright dirty! They kicked us much more than Leeds had done – and that was a game where you expected a lot of contact. They also kicked us more than any Scottish team who were at Ibrox during the entire season. They booted lumps out of us. They were one rough, tough team that night. They didn't miss us at all and it was the most physical game we faced at Ibrox that season. I can only think that they expected us to adopt these tactics against them – we didn't. What they did was retaliate first, as the old saying goes. But while they kicked us they also played. At times in the first hour of that game we were chasing shadows. They were simply superb.

But when we had possession thay attacked us. Whatever was needed to regain the ball then that's what they did. If they had to kick one of us then they did that. If they had to barge someone off the ball then they did that. They stooped to anything until they had the ball and then came the switch. In an amazing transformation they became the team we had expected from the start, a free-flowing football team with players who stuck the ball around the field effortlessly. They showed these two contrasting faces that night and even our most loyal fans in the near 42,000 crowd must have thought that our dreams of reaching the final were going to end. It really was that important in the opening game to get a result which would keep you in contention.

If we had allowed Marseille to leave with a victory then some of our later games at home could have become meaningless and the crock of gold the club expected would not have materialised. We were down 2-0 after just under an hour and the game was slipping beyond our reach. Alen Boksic, the Croatian striker who was one of their truly outstanding players, scored after half an hour and then Rudi Voller, an old opponent of mine, snatched a second after 57 minutes. We had started without Ally McCoist and Ian Ferguson and were so hard-pressed for fit players – and Scottish players at that – that we had Davie Dodds on the bench!

90

Yet it was from that bench where Doddsy was acting as a father figure to a bunch of our kids as well as goalkeeper Ally Maxwell that our salvation arrived. I missed the fightback because I had been forced to limp off with an injury after the start of the second half. Young Steven Pressley took over and did well in a European debut but even his performance was eclipsed by Gary McSwegan, who stepped from the bench in the 78th minute and had scored with a header just 60 seconds later!

It was an incredible goal, with Alexei Mikhailichenko crossing magnificently from the left. As the French defenders followed Mark Hateley, young Gary came in from the right to send a looping header beyond the reach of the Marseille 'keeper Fabien Barthez. That set Ibrox alight and suddenly the French champions were on the ropes. Mark Hateley scored a brave goal with a low near post header two minutes later and in the closing stages Marseille's veteran coach Raymond Goethals pushed on extra defenders to allow his team to hang on to a lead which quarter of an hour earlier had seemed unassailable. It was a dramatic end to the game and a lifeline for us. We got out of jail that night and in the dressing-room afterwards we all knew that. And yet it was more than just an escape because it was a performance which underlined the defiance of our players – a quality the other sides began to fear.

The great thing about the new system was that the game was over. Each team had one point and the two away goals Marseille had scored had no bearing on the second clash we had against them in April. Before then we had to play the Russians away from home and then Bruges away from home and then at Ibrox in the only back-to-back clash we had in our group.

Two weeks later, though, we played in one of Rangers' strangest European ties – in Bochum in Germany, where

CSKA were asked to play their first supposedly 'home' game. The cruel Moscow winters which brought a league shutdown in Russia also forced UEFA to find other venues for CSKA to use during their Champions' League run. That's why we ended up in a small town in Germany, not too far from Dusseldorf, a couple of weeks before Christmas. It was our first away game and we knew it was vital that we took at least a point from the Russians, particularly as they had lost narrowly to Bruges in Belgium in their opener. The Nigerian striker Daniel Amokachi had scored the one goal of that game and so CSKA were the only team without a point.

The Russians, we knew, would not have any kind of major support but, still, the club tried to limit the number of our fans who would travel. The fear of trouble is always there in Europe even though the security set up at Ibrox and the precautions taken by the club have ensured that over the past half dozen years or more we have not suffered from any hooliganism by any of our supporters. This time, of course, there was a complication because of the number of army camps within striking distance of the venue. Controlling the army fans was going to be just that little bit more difficult. The club expected a few thousand fans to turn up – nine thousand people were in the Bochum stadium that night and by far the bulk of them wore our colours! The Russians had some support – also from the Army – from Berlin. Some locals came along but it was a party night for our fans – and the result gave them a chance to celebrate.

I missed the game because I had failed to shake off the injury I suffered against Marseille. But Ian Ferguson was back and Ally McCoist was back too, and while I was missing and we still had other injury worries, it was Fergie who scored after just quarter of an hour – and that goal was enough to leave us at the top of the group along with Marseille who defeated Bruges 3-0 in the Stade Velodrome.

They were ahead on goal difference but we were still in there as we looked towards our third game which was scheduled to be played in March in Belgium.

As for the worries over crowd trouble there was not a hint of that despite the huge numbers of fans who 'follow followed' the lads that night. They sang and they cheered on the team and they swopped scarves for Russian army hats and they celebrated – how they celebrated. I knew just as did the other lads who had played that night that we had given them a night to remember. We had also given them a growing feeling that after the stutter against Marseille at Ibrox we were once again on course for some success in Europe. The glory of the double win over Leeds and now this important win away from home was enough to capture their imaginations. It had been a long, long time since they had had a team go this distance in the European Cup without a defeat . . . too long.

All of us just wanted to prolong that run even though most of us were nervous about looking too far ahead in case we became over-confident and tripped ourselves up. Not that there is ever much chance of that kind of thing happening when Walter Smith and Archie Knox are about. Any signs that any of us might be a little complacent and a few well chosen words bring us back to earth. But we knew that we were on course and that our first appearance in the Champions' League was not going to be a let-down for our supporters.

My only worry was that my personal injury problems persisted and while I returned before Christmas I went out again and when the game in Bruges came around I was back receiving treatment . . .

Again, though, without myself, Ian Ferguson and Trevor Steven the lads rose to the heights once more. Again there were warnings of possible crowd trouble. Again our supporters travelled in their thousands. And, again they behaved superbly. The way they backed the side was magnificent. All of us talked about that during the European run and we knew that we could not let them down. They spent so much and dreamed about our success so much that they were willing us through in some of the matches.

The support was like an extra man in the Olympic Stadium in Bruges that night – and we needed them in the opening part of the game when the Belgians hurled themselves forward into attack after attack which we survived until eventually losing a goal close to the half hour mark. Their Polish international Tomasz Dzuibinski scored after we had failed to clear one of their raids. Somehow, though, that goal lifted us. The way the team came back was incredible. For almost the entire second half it was Rangers who looked like the home team and time after time the lads made chances which should have brought the equaliser – there was a marvellous header from Dave McPherson which everyone – big Dave especially – was sure was going in. Somehow their veteran 'keeper Dany Verlinden reached the ball to save it on the line. It was an inspired night for the Bruges 'keeper who was given a pain-killing injection on the field to keep him in the game. He saved them. As well as the header from Dave there was a try from Stuart McCall – the man of the match that night – which he stopped. Watching the game, I began to fear that he would defy us on his own. Then Pieter Huistra stepped in with a goal quarter of an hour from the end and we gained a draw.

That had been a particularly difficult game for the team because Bruges had crashed in Marseille and they needed a home win to re-establish themselves as potential finalists and to make certain that their last game at home against Marseille could still retain some interest.

94

Richard Gough with team-mate Mark Hateley and the Scottish Cup. Hateley was one of the players who helped influence Gough on diet and fitness after the front man's experience in Italy (Evening Times)

Two Souness signings from England – Nigel Spackman and Richard Gough – close in on former Aberdeen midfielder Paul Mason, with Brian Irvine the on-deck spectator (Evening Times)

*Grim-faced, Richard Gough arrives in Glasgow Airport from Genoa
and the World Cup finals. An early brush with Roxburgh . . .*
(Evening Times)

Happier times for the Rangers skipper when Roxburgh made him captain of his country. Here they are together at a training session (Evening Times)

A training wall of 'dummy' players tests Scotland stars Gordon Durie, Kevin Gallacher, Brian McClair and Gary McAllister in Sweden. Roxburgh likes the dummies – they don't talk back! (Evening Times)

As skipper at the European Championship finals in Sweden Gough rises to beat the German striker Karl-Heinz Riedle in this duel (John Young/Evening Times)

Lee Chapman outjumps Richard Gough and John Brown in the first match against Leeds United, October 1992 (John Young/ Evening Times)

Marseille v Rangers: Gough and Boli, April 1993 (John Young/
Evening Times)

Marseille v Rangers: Richard Gough challenges keeper Fabien Barthez,
April 1993 (John Young/Evening Times)

No matter which way they tried, Gough could not score. Rangers v CSKA Moscow, April 1993 (John Young/
Evening Times)

It's a bloody heartbreak: Rangers skipper Richard Gough, despite his head wound, finds time to console striker Ally McCoist after the final whistle against CSKA Moscow at Ibrox, April 1993
(Evening Times)

*Richard Gough hides his tears as McCall offers a hand to Ally McCoist
after the 0-0 draw with CSKA Moscow at Ibrox, April 1993*
(John Young/Evening Times)

For ourselves we had to build on the result against the Russians for much the same reasons. We could not afford to lose – and we didn't. I think the changing face of European football was underlined that night. The Champions' League lends itself to positive football away from home. If we had been playing a normal tie then we might have been happy to settle for a 1-0 defeat from Bruges, knowing that we had a return game at Ibrox to come. In the league situation we wanted at least a point from the match and we went after it.

Afterwards the Bruges captain Franky van der Elst remarked in wonderment: 'The Scots just do not accept defeat. This is their greatest quality. They have a spirit which we could not subdue. We should have been warned by the way they came back to save the game against Marseille in Glasgow – but we just did not believe that they could do that away from their own stadium. But they did and while we have some slim hopes left the group will surely lie between the French and the Scots . . .'

He had summed up the attitude which ran through our entire campaign – these players simply would not give up. Even when everything looked to be against them they did not accept that they would lose. There was a feeling of resolve in the dressing-room, on the training ground and into the games, and that carried us through difficult times. Bruges was one of them – and its importance became even more evident after the match when we all heard the score from Berlin where Marseille were playing the 'homeless' Russians.

They had not rediscovered the magic they had shown when beating Barcelona *en route* to the last eight – though we had found them troublesome, at times, in Bochum when we had met them. But they had lost to us there in Germany and they had lost to Bruges in Belgium in their first match.

Against Marseille in Berlin – where UEFA had now based them – no one gave them a chance. When Abedir Pele pushed the French champions in front after 27 minutes it looked even more odds-on that they would coast to victory. They didn't. Illshat Fayzulin, the baby-faced wonder boy of Russian soccer, equalised and the game ended with Marseille on the ropes and with ourselves and the French sitting on the same points' total and the group balanced delicately.

By this time, of course, the new-style tournament was being hailed as a major success. Our game against Marseille had drawn TV viewing figures even greater than *Coronation Street*! And the opening eight games were seen by 350 million viewers. It was tremendous to be a part of the success and those figures convinced me still more that the attacking play the league rewarded was exactly what the paying public wanted to see.

Now we had the return against the Belgian champions to look forward to and I desperately wanted to be fit for that match. It was touch and go for me. I missed the next three games, the cup-tie at Arbroath and two Premier League games against St Johnstone and Hibs. But for Bruges I decided to play, as did Andy Goram who had been sidelined with me since the match in Belgium. Ian Ferguson was still missing and I knew that our resources were stretched thin, so while I was not 100 per cent ready I decided to play. I was glad that I did because on the night we needed all our experience to sweep aside the challenge from the Belgian side – in a match which was made extra hard for us when Mark Hateley was sent off. We could not believe the decision made by the Polish referee. But the red card was shown.

Rudi Cossey, the giant defender of Bruges, had been told to man-mark our striker. When he more or less put a neck lock on Mark, he retaliated and pushed him off. The referee saw Mark's reaction but missed the earlier foul against him. And so he brandished his red card and Cossey escaped without punishment. At that time – it was right on half time – we were leading through an Ian Durrant goal which had come just minutes before the sending-off. If Mark had still been on the field then we would have been looking at the possibility of a comfortable win when we talked things over in the dressing-room at half time. But without him and facing a full 45 minutes of a high-pressure European game with only ten men our thoughts were more of survival.

They moved still further in that direction when Bruges equalised through their 26-year-old midfield man Lorenzo Staelens, one of the half dozen Belgian international stars in their side. As van der Elst had predicted so accurately in his summing up of the Rangers team, we did not give up – but we knew that we were in trouble. Possibly because we felt deeply the injustice of the red card given to Mark Hateley our determination to hold on for a draw – and, if possible, nick a win – was stronger than ever. We dug in, refusing to allow Bruges to get too much benefit from their extra man and in 71 minutes we were rewarded. It was then that Scott Nisbet struck with a little help from the elements! Call the goal lucky if you wish. Call it anything you want but, for us, it was the goal we deserved for the work we had put into the two matches. Dany Verlinden, who had defied us in Belgium, misjudged Nissy's try. He came off his line and then when the ball bounced on a dry piece of ground in the box he tried to go back. It rose high over his head and then dropped into goal . . . it was the winner we needed. And it made up for the bad luck we had suffered in the first leg when we should have won the game. No matter how they go in, all of them count and that one counted for a lot.

While we had been having our problems, Marseille had been avenging themselves against CSKA. The Russians were destroyed in the Stade Velodrome as Franck Sauzee scored a hat-trick in a six-goal romp. The French side had been three goals ahead by half time and the Russians could not handle their attacks.

Now the stage was set for a head to head between ourselves and the team who had been named favourites to win the trophy. They were our next opponents and we had to travel to their seaport home knowing that we would be asked to handle a crowd which would attempt to intimidate us as well as a team who had won their two home games and scored nine goals without losing any. It was the most formidable task we had been asked to take on and yet we felt good about our prospects. Don't ask me why. The omens seemed set against us. Marseille had beaten us in a pre-season friendly and followed that up by outplaying us for an hour at Ibrox in our first European Cup clash. They were looked on as near enough invincible at home and yet as the game approached we had a growing feeling that we could surprise them. Perhaps it was the confidence we had gained from the matches we had played so far. Perhaps it was a natural way to feel when you are enjoying success on all fronts. By the time we travelled to Marseille we were in the Scottish Cup final and we had beaten Aberdeen in a vital Premier League game to just about clinch our fifth successive title. Europe had been a bonus and now we looked for the big pay-off against the French champions. The propaganda they had been pumping out didn't worry us. They wrote us off and their coach Raymond Goethals was more than uncomplimentary about the style of football we played. Then, too, they made things hard for our fans to get to the game. They agreed one allocation of tickets and then cut back on the numbers. It took long, hard negotiations by the club to get any tickets at all from them. Everything was done to unsettle us – but, by this time, nothing was going to do that.

I still remember saying to the lads in the dressing-room before the game that we had to be as hard and as physical in our approach as they had been in the first game at Ibrox. I felt that was our only chance. We were going to be without Mark Hateley because he was suspended for our last two games and that was a blow because we knew Marseille feared him, so we had to surprise them in other ways. One was to take a physical approach just as they had done at Ibrox. That had surprised us then. We had been taken aback by the ferocity of their tackling, by the way they harried us in midfield and how their defenders snapped at our forwards' heels while their forwards checked back to help.

No one, of course, was expected to do that at the Stade Velodrome – visiting teams were meant to be too frightened to upset the partisan fans. But it didn't matter to us. We had to keep our hopes of reaching the finals alive and only a draw – or, of course, a win – could do that. By now it had gone almost all the way and if either ourselves or Marseille won this vital clash then it was all over – the winners then went into the final in the Olympic Stadium in Munich where they would meet the mighty AC Milan who had strolled to success in the other group.

A draw would leave us level on points with Marseille who were facing a possibly hazardous trip to Bruges while we were at home to CSKA in our final match. The fact that we had home advantage might give us a slight edge . . . if that became the scenario. First of all, however, we had to get something against Marseille.

So in the dressing-room that night, as tension built we made up our minds that we would dig in, that we would tackle just as they had tackled in Glasgow and that we would give better than we got in any battles for possession. We were more fired up for that game than for any other – and when we took the field and began to give some of their players the message they didn't like it. How they moaned! How they complained! How they protested to the referee!

At Ibrox we had taken our lumps – in the Stade Velodrome they started to look for protection from the match officials. They just didn't like it one little bit – and while we lost a goal in the 17th minute we knew that they were more rattled than the 1-0 scoreline at that time might have suggested. We had been shocked at Ibrox by how they played. But I think we really caught them out even more because they had expected us to be soft touches. The other two teams had been beaten before the first half was over – they looked at us and thought we would be the same. We were supposed to be cannon fodder for them. When we gave them the message a few times they lost the poise they had shown in all their other games. As in Bruges, when we went behind – it was another goal from Franck Sauzee who finished as the tournament's top goal-getter – we refused to give in. Seven minutes into the second half Ian Durrant struck a marvellous angled shot past Barthez to put us level and in the end we might have won that game. Sure, they came back at us, but we handled everything they could hit us with. I look back on that as one of our best ever performances even though we did not win the game. What we did do was go into the lion's den and emerge with a reputation which was enhanced right across the Continent.

In Berlin Bruges won 2-1 and now for the first time our fate was in the hands of others. If Bruges could defeat or draw with Marseille while we won our last match at home against CSKA, then we would be finalists. But it depended on Bruges, no matter what we did in front of our own fans . . .

We went into that last match still without Mark and against CSKA who defended in their own penalty box deeper than the other teams we had met. This was a serious blow. On the night we could not score while Alen Boksic scored for Marseille after just two minutes.

We ended in second place in the group as thousands of fans wept in the Ibrox stands.

It was a sad end to a campaign which had begun eight months earlier but we had the consolation of knowing that in *ten* games in Europe we had not suffered a single defeat. Only Marseille and AC Milan could boast a similar statistic at that stage – the sole defeat for the Italians came in the final when Marseille won the trophy.

You look back now and you think that perhaps you should have won the last game – but in the end that would have made no difference to how things were concluded. Marseille would still have gone on to the final. I do wish that we had had a chance to play in a semi-final – that's something which has now been introduced to the tournament. The teams who are second in each group will play the winners of the other group. Just one game on the ground of the group winners. The winners in these semi-finals will go on to the final. That would have given us a crack at Milan and our supporters another opportunity to see top-class European football.

But there is no doubt in my mind that we forged a new and formidable reputation in Europe with our unbeaten run. Now we have to try to build on that. It won't be easy. It never is. Yet over the next few years we have to attempt to push our claims to being one of Europe's top teams. The Champions' League has been a huge success. In football terms it has encouraged attacking play – there was only one 0-0 draw in the matches last season and that was our last match against CSKA. Fifty-five goals were scored in the 24 games and a total of 800,000 fans attended the matches.

It's now something of which every team wants to be a part. We have tasted the new format and we liked it. So did our supporters. And, at the end of it all, it was these supporters who won praise from UEFA President Lennart Johansson, who said they showed an outstanding example to all fans in the way they gave us a standing ovation at the end of the CSKA game. He said what the players already knew – that our fans are simply the best!

CHAPTER SEVEN

The Reign of Graeme

There is no doubt in my mind that the most significant period in my time in Scottish football was the Rangers' revolution which occurred under the reign of Graeme Souness.

Love him or loathe him – and too many people around our country took the second option – no one could ignore him. Nor could they fail to see how he had revitalised the entire football scene. I was playing for one of the 'New Firm' sides when Aberdeen and Dundee United were challenging the long-established Old Firm of Rangers and Celtic in the Eighties. It was good to be a part of that, good to be in a team which was gaining success at home and abroad and, at the same time, carve out some kind of reputation and future for yourself. Rangers, then, were a sleeping giant. They were winning nothing – or next to nothing – and by the time Graeme took over in the summer of 1986 they had struggled to get a place in Europe.

Gates had slumped and the club had become a joke – but the rest of football in Scotland shouldn't have been laughing too much at Rangers' troubles. For their troubles meant a loss of income to the game, which was damaging. It was Graeme Souness, with the help of Walter Smith, who changed all of that.

Suddenly 'Ground Full' notices sprouted up around the country whenever Rangers were the visiting team. Graeme imported star names and the game in Scotland, which had been slowly withering away, had a new vitality. Graeme Souness didn't just help Rangers – though that was his clear priority – by doing that. He brought the Scottish game back to life and gave it a new prosperity.

I knew Graeme as a team-mate from international matches and I had been in Mexico at the World Cup finals when he was captain of the squad. When I was just breaking into the team he was good to me. He was one of the senior players who went out of his way to help me relax at Scotland get togethers. I know that he picked up some criticism from other players for being aloof and stand-offish – but I never found him like that. With me he was helpful and welcoming and I always take people how I find them. I just never found him to be anything other than friendly . . .

When he made his first move to sign me from Dundee United I wanted to go. As well as Graeme, Walter Smith was there and we had been close from almost the first day I joined up at Tannadice. Jim McLean refused to sell me to Rangers and I ended up going to Spurs before Graeme came back in for me. I was impressed that he did so after failing to get me first time around.

I saw that as a sign of his single-mindedness. He wanted me in his team, he thought I would improve the team, and so when I was available – a year after he first wanted me – he did not hesitate. Nor did the fact that the fee had doubled inside that year-long period deter him. He could have jibbed at paying that kind of money but he didn't. It was a hefty premium he was asked to fork out but Graeme felt I was a player he wanted to be a part of *his*

Rangers team and so he paid the money and took me there.

I liked that about him. I also admired how blunt and straight-talking he was. He was a strong-willed man and you were never in any doubt where you stood with him. He was the kind of man I admired. Single-minded. Ambitious. Utterly determined to be a success. I always had the impression that Graeme knew exactly what he wanted. From his team. From himself. From football. And from life. Not very much was allowed to stand in his way either . . .

You will have realised by now that I am a great admirer of Walter Smith and more than that I like to think that we are close on a personal level because of the length of our relationship. Graeme and Walter made a marvellous team but it needed Graeme Souness to bring about the Rangers revolution.

It needed someone with his high profile, someone with his experience outside Scotland, to lift the whole place. The bold strokes which were needed at the beginning could only have come from someone with Graeme's style and authority. For instance, he smashed the wage structure at the club making it possible to buy big name players from England. He was right to do that because it had to be done if the club were ever to fulfil its potential. Other managers would not have been as daring as Graeme. If Jim McLean had taken the job, for instance, when he was offered it some two years or so earlier, he would not have known where to start as regards wages and bonuses. He would not have been able to persuade players such as Terry Butcher and Chris Woods to join Rangers. Wee Jim would have overhauled the scouting system and he would have changed the training and the approach to coaching at the club . . . but he would not have had the courage to make the sweeping changes Graeme brought about so quickly.

Graeme did not want to take his time. He wanted success from the start and he got it. If he had failed, then it would have been the most spectacular football flop ever seen. But Graeme is never one to contemplate failure at anything. And, if you look back at the signings he made at the start you will see that he was following basic soccer principles. He got the defence right before he started working on other areas. He knew that if you make a team solid at the back then you build from there. Woods and Butcher were class acts. He wanted the best, he went for the best and he soon had a team which was difficult to defeat.

But Graeme knew that if you wanted the best team then you had to pay the best wages. Now if he had spent his entire career in Scotland he would not have known how to compete with the top clubs in England. But Graeme knew the set up at Liverpool and he had spent time in Italy, so he knew the going rate as it were. Eventually Graeme had turned Rangers into the biggest team in Britain. He bought quality players – almost all of them proven winners – he paid them good wages and he brought the club success. In turn his policies guaranteed sell out crowds at Ibrox and massive season ticket sales which brought such a demand that the club still have a waiting list!

Of course Graeme had problems. His style of management ensured that there would always be controversy surrounding him and the club. He clashed with authority frequently and he fell foul of football's establishment. I think that happened through a combination of circumstances. Scotland is a small country and a lot of the attitudes remain parochial. Graeme was constantly in the headlines and the club was the same and that brought jealousies to the surface. As long as I have been in the game in Scotland, Rangers and the Scottish Football Association seem to have been at loggerheads over one thing or another. It might be over allocation of Cup final tickets. Or over the release of players for international games. Or it could come when Graeme clashed with referees or linesmen . . .

Sometimes it could be about very little. At other times it could be serious. Always, though, there was this running battle between Graeme and the club and the authoriries. To add to all of that Graeme's type of management also brought him into conflict with the media. He would be at war with one newspaper or another. Or he would stop speaking to one TV station or a radio programme and he seemed to go from one crisis to another. Not that Graeme allowed such clashes to bother him. He seemed to take them in his stride.

There was the time of his feud with Scottish Television when he came down the tunnel at Ibrox at a time when he was banned from the dugout. He came nowhere near the dugout area. Nor did any of the players even realise he was standing there – but STV showed him standing there and landed him in further trouble with the soccer bosses. It was vindictive – but as I said at the beginning of this part of the book there was a lot of jealousy around simply because Rangers were the *biggest, wealthiest* and *most powerful* club in the country. Everyone wanted to have a go at us and often Graeme gave them the excuse to do just that.

I'm not suggesting for a moment that he was blameless. He was a very emotional person and he did get upset when decisions went against the team – but so do other managers and when they do they receive far less publicity than Graeme did.

Even in the dressing-room there were players who had problems with the way Graeme approached the job. They found him difficult and they found him demanding. Graeme made it very clear that he wanted the players to behave like professionals *all* the time. He was very hot on that kind of thing. He found it hard when people did not live up to his standards or try to behave according to the code of conduct he had been attempting to set up at Ibrox. He insisted that players should give themselves the best possible chance of performing to their full abilities each match day. He felt that sometimes some of the players didn't give themselves that chance by stepping out of line when they were away from the ground. He was hard on the younger players who did not live up to the high standards he set them – and he did set high standards. He believed that if the club was going to pay top wages then only top performances were acceptable. If performance levels dropped because of some kind of misbehaviour then he was liable to come down on the offenders like a ton of bricks. Guilty players resented that.

I did not have any problem with him that way because his attitude tended to mirror my own views. I did have a couple of barneys with him but that was natural because both of us are single-minded and know what we want. We didn't see eye to eye on everything. Graeme allowed players to express their opinions as long as they realised that 99 times out of hundred he would have the last word. I found that OK but there was one occasion when a clash of wills between us almost saw me leave Rangers. That was the last thing I wanted – it had taken me so long to get there in the first place – and yet I could have gone because I thought he had called me a 'cheat', and I wasn't going to have that from Graeme Souness or from anyone else.

It happened during the period I was having serious problems from my foot injury. It was a nightmare time for me. Some games I would feel the pain inside the first ten minutes. Or maybe it would take twenty minutes or half an hour, but it almost always came and it would be agony. And while I knew this was getting to Graeme, that was not my main concern. I was much more worried about getting a proper diagnosis of the injury than I was about his feelings. There were games when I felt I was going to be fit to play and then had to come off during the match. Other times the pain was so severe that I couldn't even take the field. Quite simply, Graeme was a manager who wanted his best team on the park every game. If he wanted you to play even though you were suffering from a little knock then you played. That was it. His word went. But this injury was more serious than the usual niggles players can put up with. I was worrying about the damage which might be done to my career because this was genuinely a mystery injury. No one could find out what was wrong with me. The longer it went on the more I began to believe that my career could end because no one could give a proper diagnosis. It was a big, big problem for me and it lasted for a long, long time. I was playing in real pain and in almost every match and nothing could ease that for me. Padding didn't help. Neither did strappings. More often than not I had to bite the bullet and get on with things. It was not easy.

Graeme's attitude made it even harder for me. He was never one to make allowances for injury – his own or anyone else's. There was an impatience about him when it came to injuries, as if he didn't think your body should let you down. My clash with him came about because of his own frustrations and my personal worries. Looking at the situation now it seems incredible that it could have ended my career with Rangers – but it almost did! In fact, given the circumstances, it was the worst period I have known since returning to Scottish football.

You have to understand that I was regularly being asked to go through the pain barrier. Sometimes the pain was just a nagging thing, other times it blazed into pure agony. But, always, it was there. It was unrelenting and because it was on the sole of my foot between my toes there was no escaping it. Eventually the trouble was found to be something called 'Morton's Neuroma' and I required two operations to rid myself of the problem. The first – they were both in London – dealt with one neuroma but the trouble persisted and the specialist found another which was also removed. Since then I have been free from trouble with that problem. Anyhow, it all came to a head one night we played Arsenal in a challenge game at Ibrox. It was a bitterly cold night and I had to come off at half time because of the foot and the pain I was getting from it. We lost the game and afterwards I was on the treatment table – my customary spot during all of this crisis – and Graeme came in and looked at me. He said something like, 'I think you're at it.' Walter Smith was there and the physio Phil Boersma and I could not believe what I had just heard.

Nor did I know how I was supposed to react to that kind of allegation. I mean, there I was in the treatment room worrying over an injury which I believed was threatening my career and my manager was accusing me of cheating. It was ridiculous. Of course it was all down to the fact that we had lost the game and Graeme was never the best loser but this remark hurt. I did not know what to say. Neither did Walter or Phil. I just got off the treatment table, walked out of the room and slammed the door. My mind was in a turmoil and I thought to myself, 'That's it. My time here is over'. I just couldn't see any future with the club I had always dreamed of joining.

The next morning I went into Ibrox prepared for some kind of showdown. I was convinced that at some stage of the day I would be asking for a transfer. Not because I ever wanted to leave Rangers – but because I could not work with a manager who thought I was trying to cheat him or the club. I knew that if I had a confrontation with Graeme over this then I'd be off. That was guaranteed. One major row with Graeme and the player involved was very quickly off the premises. He made no secret of that and, to be honest, he couldn't because we had seen it happen so often in the past. It had to be Graeme's way and he would not brook interference or rebellion from any of his players. I was hopelessly confused by now. I didn't want to leave Ibrox – but, at the same time, I could not see any way out of my situation. Basically, I was not prepared to allow Graeme to criticise me unfairly – and equally I knew that he would never accept me telling him that. It was the classic stand off – and the ending seemed to have been written in advance if past history was anything to go by.

When I got to the ground I expected to be called upstairs for a chat. If not, then I was ready to ask to see the manager and sort out the situation. Somehow or other, though, neither thing happened. I think it was because that night we had a Burns' Supper at the club which was hosted by the chairman and so the problem was put on the back burner. I put off asking to see him and left it to see what he would do. When nothing happened I decided I would stay away from the Burns' Supper. I didn't see much point in going along to that if I was not going to be a part of the team for very much longer. I just thought to myself, 'Leave it until tomorrow and then the transfer will be put in place.' It was not the best of times for me, not knowing what the future was going to bring. But I realised that nothing I could do was going to influence the final outcome. The ball was in Graeme's court.

Then later that day I had second thoughts about the Burns' Supper. I thought to myself that this was the chairman's function, it was his little party for the players and that he had absolutely nothing to do with my row with

Graeme. So I went along that night even though I was still simmering over the after-match comment which had hurt and angered me the previous night.

Then something happened which was totally unexpected – and, for Graeme, totally out of character. At the beginning of the function Graeme got to his feet and said: 'By the way I have got to apologise to a certain player because of some very unfair remarks I made to him last night.'

He didn't name me or anything like that – but, then, he wouldn't because he would never want it to look as if he was losing face or backing down to one of his players. I knew straight away that this was the biggest peace offering I would ever get. For Graeme to apologise was unusual – for him to apologise in public was possibly unique.

I don't know what happened but I think maybe Walter had something to do with it. Graeme had probably said to him that the business with me had to be sorted out. Knowing me, Walter would have told him that I would not back down and would probably take a walk rather than be branded a cheat or stand accused of letting the club down in some way. After all it was not the kind of accusation that he would have taken from a manager when he was still a player. By being similar to him in so many ways this would have turned into a contest of wills and I would have lost because a manager always holds the aces in any showdown with a player. I would have been sold and that was that.

All of this was going through my mind as Graeme then added: 'The player knows what I'm talking about. And I was really out of order with him after the game last night.' Now everyone is looking at each other because none of the other lads had a clue to what was going on. I hadn't told anyone. I hadn't wanted to be moaning and groaning about the dressing-room because of a row with the gaffer. This was between him and me. No one else knew the scenario. That was the one major row I had with Graeme and it ended at the Burns' Supper that night. Nothing else was said. Nothing else had to be said. Other than that I didn't have a problem with Graeme. I've been upset at some of the problems he has had at Anfield since he went back there. I do hope things work out for him.

It had been a major shock when he quit the club. I received a call one night from an English journalist telling me that Graeme was going to join Liverpool. This was the night before the official announcement was made and I found it hard to believe.

I did not think that Graeme would ever have wanted to leave the club. I called another newspaper pal in London and he told me it was true. Within 24 hours the world knew what was happening. I can still remember the Press Conference that day when Graeme said his piece and then walked out of the Blue Room. I saw him at the top of the staircase and he told me, 'All the best', and I said the same to him and he added, 'Make sure and win the title'. That was it. He was gone. He was almost crying. This tough, often ruthless man, was close to tears. It was a very emotional moment for him. He was very upset and it showed in that private moment when few other people were around. I felt for him because it was obviously a decision which had taken a lot of thought and a lot of heartache to reach.

This was his team. His club. This was a side he had moulded in his image almost. To walk away from all he had achieved must have taken a lot out of him. It was a shock to the players. Normally at a club when a manager is going to leave or going to be sacked then you get some feeling about what is about to happen. This, though, came out of the blue. After all Graeme was a director as well as the manager. He had shares in the club. He had created the new Rangers. He had signed most of us. And, unlike most managers, he had the job for as long as he wanted it.

It has to be said that there were mixed emotions among the players. Some had not got on with Graeme and so a change of manager might favour them. But to a man, they all agreed that the Rangers revolution could never have taken place without him.

He gave up a lot for the club. His marriage broke up and I know what he must have gone through at that time. He had all the problems of running Rangers as well as his personal problems and he put Rangers first. People who criticise Graeme Souness should keep that in mind.

I think he was unhappy with me for a comment I made at the time he left – or when Walter was appointed – but it was taken out of context. I said something to the effect that Walter had been doing most of the work on the training ground in any case. That was interpreted as a dig at Graeme. It wasn't. The other part of the statement saying that Graeme had been the major figure at the club and the main man in its rebirth was ignored. Managers delegate work on the training ground – Graeme did that with Walter. Now Walter does it with Archie Knox. It's the way of things with a big club.

No slur was intended because I know what Graeme Souness gave to Rangers and I remain eternally grateful that he gave me the chance to be involved with the club.

CHAPTER EIGHT

Walter Takes Over – and a New Era Begins

Before that very eventful and emotional Press Conference took place the Chairman, David Murray, asked to speak to me privately. Straight away he asked me, 'What do you think?' and that was all he said. Just those four words. So then I had to ask him if it was true that Graeme was going to Liverpool and taking over there as manager for the following season.

He said that was right and then followed up by asking what the reaction would be from the players. They were all off so there was no way I could answer for them but I said simply, 'As far as I'm concerned if he is going to leave the club and everyone knows that then he should go immediately. Waiting around for next season won't help Rangers any.'

The Chairman replied: 'I'm glad you said that because his feet are not going to touch the floor going out of here.' Then came the 64,000 dollar question. 'Who would you like to have in charge of the club?' It was almost as if he was saying to me, 'Who would you give the job to if you were in my position?' I was slightly taken aback, but not too much because that is typical of the Chairman. He is a man who

115

asks a lot of questions, gets the answers and then weighs up any given situation after taking stock of the different viewpoints he may get. None of which would necessarily change his mind if it was already made up on some important issue. But he had asked me and so I just told him: 'There's only one man for the job and that's Walter Smith.'

He immediately asked if the players would be happy with that appointment and I assured him that they would all be delighted. After that he asked me if there was anyone else I thought could handle the job – like, if you had to make another choice, who would come into the picture? I told him that I thought Ray Wilkins would do a good job and he looked at me and answered: 'That's interesting – but you were right the first time. Walter will be the new manager.'

This was a week before the official announcement was made and he asked me to keep the whole thing under wraps – which I did. I realised, though, that Walter had a major job on his hands to win the title. It was so close to the end of the season, the race was tight and we had injury problems – problems which intensified as the season reached its climax. If we had lost that title in those circumstances then no one at the club would have blamed Walter for the failure. Nor could anyone have justified blaming him – though a few might have done just that. There would have been the odd supporter or two who would have said we would have taken the title if Graeme Souness had remained in the job. That is the way of things . . .

So it is important that Walter did clinch that first title. The sad thing for me was that I could not help him do it. Firstly I was suspended for the game against St Mirren at Paisley and had to watch as the team struggled a little before young Sandy Robertson scored two minutes from the end. That kept us a point ahead of Aberdeen with two games left

116

and with the Pittodrie team coming to Ibrox on the last day of the season. Then I joined the Scotland squad which was going to San Marino but was sent home because I was feeling unwell. I was in bed for three days, running a temperature, and was then sent to hospital where doctors took blood tests and found out that I was suffering from hepatitis. I was therefore ruled out of the last two games against Motherwell and Aberdeen.

Walter came to see me in hospital and he could not believe what had happened. Here was a club losing a manager and now a captain at the most crucial period of a season. When we lost to Motherwell at Fir Park we found ourselves facing up to the fact that we now had to beat Aberdeen at home to win the title. A draw was suddenly enough for them as our injury position worsened by the day. Walter was left patching up his team, patching and praying at the same time, I think, as we headed for that showdown. Terry Hurlock finished up playing left-back and John Brown played when he was injured. It was nowhere near our strongest team but Mark Hateley did the business and we won. Lying in my hospital bed listening to the radio I felt a great sense of relief for the lads and for Walter himself. He needed that title as a springboard for a managerial career which was now set to take off. The lads were so utterly professional that day. They reacted so positively to the changeover at the top and to the injuries which had forced so many changes in the side.

From then on there have been few, if any, problems. People outside the club have to remember that we were not getting a completely new manager. Walter had been with the club since Graeme's arrival and he had worked closely with the players, so the switch at the top didn't upset the structure too much. Now Walter has grown in stature in the job. Whereas he was known mainly in Scotland when he took over he has earned himself a much bigger profile over the past few seasons. Last season especially won him an increased reputation in England and right across Europe. None of that came easily. It had to be earned and Walter has worked hard at being a successful Rangers manager.

In some ways the transition must have been easy for him because he had worked at the club for so long with Graeme and the *big* change – from the small club atmosphere of Dundee United to Rangers – had already been accomplished. Yet he did have to handle the full glare of publicity and he had to take over from a manager who had brought the club success. When Graeme took over the club had been in a bad way. He turned it round, the support came back and success became second nature. Walter had a hard, hard job to keep that going. It's a tribute to him that he has not only kept the success story alive, he has outstripped Graeme. He was in charge when we ended the Scottish Cup jinx which had haunted the club for too many years – and that was the only domesic trophy Graeme could not win. Then last season he guided us to the 'treble' and took us through Europe undefeated.

The 'treble' pushes him up among the truly *great* Rangers managers. I think supporters see him up there with Struth and Symon and Waddell and he has achieved all of that in his own way. He has not copied Graeme's style of management though after working so closely with him at the club he could have been forgiven if he had borrowed a little from the man who preceded him.

Quite simply, Walter is a different kind of manager than Graeme was. For a start, he is much more of a diplomat than Graeme could ever be. He does not go out of his way to seek confrontation with people – be it with his own players or outside the club. Graeme relished a bit of that. Things were black and white with him. You were either with him or against him. There was no halfway house. At times that was not a bad thing but Walter, while he holds views as strongly as Graeme ever did, will step back a little and consider all sides of a question and try to assess what fall-out there may be before jumping in. He is not the type of man who will seek confrontation, but he won't walk away from it either if it comes up. If a player forces a showdown with him then the player will lose. A few players have tried him out and lost and they are no longer at the club. Walter is a very strong person but he still maintains a good relationship with the players. He is closer to the lads than Graeme was latterly. He mixes with us – but we still know he is the Boss.

I think, early on, people must have realised the respect he enjoys among other coaches and managers when Archie Knox accepted his offer to become number two at the club. He left Manchester United when they were in the final of the European Cup Winners' Cup to come to Rangers – and one of the major reasons for that was to team up with Walter. The club has its own lure but Archie wanted to work with Walter and he became a similar buffer between the manager and the players as Walter was when Graeme Souness was in charge. Indeed, not only Archie but also the rest of the backroom staff underline the respect Walter has won for himself in the game. Davie Dodds, Billy Kirkwood and John McGregor all work on the same wavelength as Walter himself and you can see young players start to come through the system – something Walter has worked hard to achieve. It has taken time but the wait has been worth while when you see some of the talent now emerging.

Probably one of the most difficult jobs Walter has as a manager – apart from satisfying the never-ending thirst of the fans for success and more success – is in man-management. He is, as it happens, a superb tactician and we found that out in Europe last season! But on a domestic level we don't need tactics' talks week after week, mainly because we know our opponents so well from playing each other four times or more every season. So on a game-to-game basis in Scotland it is more about motivation and he motivates players better than any other manager I have played for. He knows how to get the best out of players without resorting to the threats and the bullying Jim McLean used at Tannadice. Of course, we were all experienced enough to know that if we are not playing well then we will be out of the team. Walter has a powerful squad of players and that, in itself, ensures that no one wants to drop his standards.

A major problem, of course, is that good players, and I'm talking here of players who would walk into any other Premier League team, can find themselves sitting out big games. It's a nice problem for a manager to have in one way – it emphasises the strength in depth he has at his disposal. For a player, though, it's different. Yet Walter manages to keep players happy. He does it through understanding how a player must feel. He has a concern for his players and you can see how that is reciprocated. Players have left the club while Walter has been in charge but there have never been any recriminations – no hint of bad feeling, no lingering resentments, nothing to suggest that a player has left under a cloud. Any sales have come at a time which has been right for the club and for the players involved. No one has ever been frozen out. If someone is out of the team or even out of the squad for a big game then he has been taken aside and been told why the decision has been made. Players appreciate that. Possibly Walter watched bust-ups between Jim McLean and players and then Graeme and players and resolved to play it differently when he became a boss himself. It certainly seems that way because you won't find anyone in football with a bad word to say about Walter

Smith. He is genuinely respected by all of us at Ibrox and by people with other clubs too.

I think there was perhaps a body of opinion which questioned how Walter could step out of Graeme's shadow and be his own man. Personally I didn't see any shadow over Walter Smith. He has been his own man ever since I have known him, even when he was in the number two role. Certainly Graeme's personality and reputation was important to the club when the partnership kicked off at Ibrox but Walter was never looked upon as being just a 'number two' to Graeme. He was always much more than that and Graeme acknowledged that himself on many occasions.

Last season was a difficult one for all of us because of the number of games we had to face – and the number of high pressure games at that! Somehow Walter hit on the right formula to get us through all of it. Towards the end of the season he and Archie cut right back on training. Now both of them work us hard normally, but recognising the pressures we were all under they gave us a lot of freedom and the players responded by giving them the results they wanted. Not too many managers would have been able to hit the right note in these circumstances – but Walter did. He has also contributed to the comradeship which exists between the lads. He has taken all of us out for lunch at times after big games or even before big games – and the last two years we have spent a week in Monaco. All of these things help build a good feeling among the players and Walter has encouraged that. Again, it has paid off on the field.

In the transfer market, too, Walter has shown tremendous judgment. Where would we have been in the last couple of seasons without Andy Goram, Stuart McCall and David Robertson – the three players who were his first signings for the club? They have become so important to

121

Rangers. Similarly the buying of Duncan Ferguson has demonstrated that Walter is always ready to back his judgment. Four million pounds is a lot of money and Rangers had to pay a premium to prise the player away from Dundee United. But I'm sure he will prove as valuable as the other buys I have mentioned and over ten years he'll only have cost the club £400,000 a year. He could turn out a bargain buy!

I owe Walter a lot. He has helped me all through my career, from the time when I was just starting out as a raw youngster with Dundee United until the present day. I'm not talking with hindsight when I say I knew he would be a good manager for Rangers Football Club because I said it from the first day. As well as the abilities I have mentioned, Walter also has a deep regard and affection for the club and a respect for its traditions. He is not often dragged into controversy but if the club is being criticised then Walter will act. He will not stand by and have Rangers bad-mouthed and he will not allow anyone to criticise his players. He does not do that to players of other clubs and clearly he does not believe it should happen.

For me that adds to the dignity of the man as manager and the club as the top side in the country. I know from personal experience that he will always defend his players. When I was criticised by Scotland manager Andy Roxburgh for declaring myself unfit before a European Championship game in Switzerland – an incident I have dealt with in an earlier chapter – Walter defended me. He knew the truth and he made certain that everyone knew the truth about that particular incident. I was grateful to him for that.

Rangers fans can be grateful to him for many other reasons. For bringing them more success than they might have dreamed possible . . . for making the club one of the most respected in Europe . . . for bringing star names no matter the cost . . . and for working hard behind the scenes to bring a youth policy to fruition.

I think the treble pushed him into any Ibrox Hall of Fame . . . and his achievements are not over yet. Just by having Walter Smith as manager Rangers are the envy of clubs all across Europe. As one of his players all I can do is try to do my own little bit to help him to more honours and I know that's how everyone in the dressing-room feels. I told the Chairman that the players would react positively to Walter's appointment and I think I've been proved right!

CHAPTER NINE

Butch and Robbo and Other Departures

There was a spell, not long after I first came back to Scotland to join Rangers, that it seemed as if there was a revolving door at the foot of the marble staircase. Players came and went and sometimes you wondered just who would be in the dressing-room when you arrived for training in the morning. There were various reasons for the turnover in staff, I suppose. The manager, Graeme Souness, was still trying to build the team he wanted and bit by bit he was getting it right in every area. Sometimes, though, if he felt that a player he had bought was not going to be right then that player was moved on . . .

Or if a player was not ready to conform to the code of conduct which Graeme had at Ibrox then he was on his bike. Quickly. Similarly, if anyone clashed with him about tactics or even questioned his approach to management then that player was on borrowed time from the moment he had challenged Graeme's authority.

There was only one *boss* at Ibrox and that was Graeme Souness and most of us accepted that. It's that way at most football clubs, though some managers would not act as swiftly or as ruthlessly as Graeme would when he felt something had to be done.

The Danish player Jan Bartram was one player who wanted to question Graeme's management style. He simply could not understand it when Graeme flew into a rage over a bad result or over something which had gone wrong on the field. He left not too long after he had signed and he claimed that he had seen Graeme boot in a television set when he flew off the handle after one game. Well, I heard a lot of shouting and saw a few cups broken but I never saw any incident with a television set and I think that's something which has been exaggerated over the years. Still, it was a good story and I suppose that's why it has survived in the many myths which surrounded Graeme's time in charge of the club. I simply don't believe it myself.

Anyhow, Jan Bartram was one of the short-term visitors. Another was Mel Sterland who came up in a £600,000 deal from Sheffield Wednesday towards the end of one season. He helped us win the title by playing in a handful of games – mostly out of position – and then he was sold in the summer to Leeds United. In all I think he played just nine games and had three appearances as sub. He was gone before any of us really got to know him. But Graeme had needed him to help win the title and then once that was done he was sold back down south where he helped Leeds get promotion and then take the championship down in England as well.

But the departures which caused most controversy at the time surrounded the leaving of Terry Butcher and Graham Roberts. Terry had been one of Graeme's initial signings from England when he first took over as manager. He had certain very basic ideas on the type of team he wanted. Quite rightly, he looked for solidity at the back and Terry and Chris Woods were early big money buys at a time when no one seriously thought that top English stars would take the high road to Scotland. Graeme proved all of them wrong.

He also wanted a big target man up front but until he finally was able to get Mark Hateley he was less successful in that quest. Colin West, Mark Falco and Kevin Drinkell all had spells in that role. None of them lasted very long.

But to many Terry Butcher was the cornerstone of the new Rangers. He was Graeme's captain and he had been terrific as a player and as a PR man for the club. There's no doubt that when Terry came to Ibrox rather than join Manchester United or Spurs, other players in England sat up and took notice. He was at the core of the Ibrox revolution which Graeme Souness started that summer of 1986 when he persuaded him to sign.

That's why when the break came it was unexpected and it brought in its wake waves of publicity. I thought at the time that it was wrong that the relationship between Graeme and Terry should end in tears as it did. And it was a shame that Terry's Rangers career finished on a sour note after four years of almost unremitting success.

He was a really good guy to have at the club, a great captain, and what he achieved at Ibrox was probably the high point of his career. I think he grew to love the club and he had this wonderful rapport with the supporters. The crowd loved him and, after all the years at Ipswich in front of small, polite crowds, he revelled in the Ibrox atmosphere. It seemed a football marriage made in heaven until early in the season 1990-91 when it all fell apart.

I have a feeling that the trouble had its roots in Terry's decision to go to the World Cup finals in Italy with England that previous summer. He had been having problems with his knee and the medical staff at Ibrox thought he would be better resting at home instead of going into the pressures of the World Cup finals. But Terry had a strong relationship with Bobby Robson who had been his club boss at Ipswich and he was a patriot. It meant a lot to him to play for his country, and while he probably knew he was running a risk of aggravating his knee trouble he went to the finals . . .

It was not a decision which could have pleased Graeme, who wanted his club captain back at full fitness that next season. So when Terry did come back and when he did look a little less than 100 per cent Graeme had a problem. And when he had a problem he met it head on. One thing about Graeme – he could never be accused of being indecisive. He was straight to the point and when he felt the team was suffering he took action. That's what he did this time and when he axed Terry it was front-page news in Glasgow.

Terry was managing to play in the games OK at the start of that season – but he was toiling for fitness and he was scarcely doing any training. It all came to a head after a match at Tannadice where big Terry scored a spectacular own goal. Our defence was not at its best and Graeme made up his mind that he had to leave Terry out. The problem he had, though, was that we were due to meet Aberdeen in the semi-final of the Skol Cup at Hampden the following midweek. It was a very difficult decision for Graeme – a lot of managers might have walked away from it, done nothing and hoped it would all come right on the night. That was not his way, however.

Twenty-four hours before the semi-final he took me aside at training and told me what he was going to do. He said that John Brown would be playing alongside me at the centre of the defence and that Terry was to be dropped because – in his words – 'the big man is struggling'. He gave me the captaincy and then he told the other players. We were all surprised because dropping a club captain for a vital semi-final clash is hardly an everyday occurrence. When we got back to the dressing-room Terry was not there. He had gone and I could understand that. It must have been an enormous blow to his pride when Graeme told him that he was to be left out.

Terry was a thorough professional and he was very conscious of the status afforded any player who is the captain of Rangers. Losing that role in such a way must have hurt him deeply. The axeing was kept under wraps until just before the match against Aberdeen. We won 1-0 – fortunately for Graeme, because, by now, the fans were questioning the decision and when we lost to Red Star Belgrade there were plenty of calls for Terry's return. The Skol Cup final was looming once again and that was an Old Firm clash with Celtic. The pressure on Graeme must have been enormous.

Then something happened between the two men that only they know the truth of. We were in the dark just as those outside the club were left guessing.

Terry was called into the manager's office for a chat – and relations between the two men had been strained to say the least since the semi-final. We were getting ready to leave for the pre-match hotel HQ when this happened. One theory was that Graeme had asked Terry if he would play for 45 minutes in a reserve match before the final to prove his fitness levels were back and that he could be risked against Celtic on the Sunday at Hampden. The outcome, in that story, was that Terry had told Graeme that he was not fit to play.

The other story was that Graeme had never asked him to play and the chat had been simply to discuss the future. Only the two of them really know what happened in that conversation but at the end of it all Terry did not play in the final.

I reckon that Terry had seen the writing on the wall. While all this was going on Graeme had completed the signing of Oleg Kuznetsov from Dynamo Kiev and the talk with Terry came after Oleg had been badly injured in just his second game.

I don't know what happened but whatever was said finished Terry as a Rangers player. If Graeme did ask Terry to play and he refused then there is no way at all Graeme would have accepted that. There would have been no way back . . . and the whole business did end in acrimony.

Luckily for Graeme we won the Skol Cup even though we had gone behind early in the second half to a Paul Elliott goal. Mark Walters equalised and then I grabbed the winner in extra time.

A few weeks later Terry was gone. He was sold to Coventry for £450,000 and took over there as player-manager. Later he lost that job and he is now with Sunderland and, obviously, he has not been able to recapture the heady days with Rangers when one trophy after another was being won. These things happen in football. As players we all know that – and some day it might happen to me. We go into the game knowing the risks.

But that does not alter my view that it was a sad end to a short but magnificent career at Ibrox. There were so many good times he and Graeme had shared that it was a tragedy when there was bitterness at the end. Yet, now that Terry has been a manager for a spell himself, he realises that tough decisions have to be made. Unhappily past glories don't help you win fresh titles. I felt a lingering sadness, though, that it had gone sour and that the revolution Terry had sparked off would now be going on without him . . .

The other major row over a player's departure was when Graham Roberts was sold to Chelsea after a dressing-room row with Graeme Souness. This time I didn't shed too many tears even though I had been partially responsible for Robbo arriving at Ibrox in the first place.

That all happened soon after I had gone to Spurs. I came back to Scotland one weekend when the Skol Cup final was on and Rangers were playing Celtic. I had decided to go to the game and I told Chrissy Waddle and Robbo my plans. They decided to come up to see the game too. They loved it and Robbo made up his mind there and then that he would like to play for Rangers because of the fantastic atmosphere which had surrounded the match – as it always does when the Old Firm meet – and I suppose because he saw that what was going to happen at Rangers was going to be very big. Also, since I had gone to White Hart Lane he had been moved into midfield from centre-back and it was not a move he enjoyed. He made it very clear that he was unhappy about playing there and eventually demanded a transfer. When that happened Graeme Souness stepped in and soon Robbo was at Rangers and playing in the position he wanted to play in – at the heart of the defence alongside Terry Butcher.

So, as you see, I had a little bit to do with Robbo becoming a Rangers player. If I had not suggested going to the Skol Cup final then he might not have begun his love affair with the fans. And if I hadn't taken his position with Spurs he might have stayed on down there . . . As Jimmy Greaves always tell us, 'It's a funny old game'.

It all sounds very simple now as I go through it in my memory but I honestly believe it was that simple. He had been toiling a little in midfield and wanted to be at the back and when it was clear he wanted to go then Spurs gave him his wish. But not without a little farewell message from the manager David Pleat who hadn't been the happiest man in the world when Robbo demanded a transfer. Pleaty said something like, 'He has kicked a few players down here so no doubt he will kick a few more up there.' I don't think Robbo liked that remark too much but off he went and a year later I joined him . . . and not too long afterwards I was given a hint of the kind of attitude he sometimes adopted. Terry Butcher broke his leg in a match and I was moved to centre-back to play alongside Graham Roberts – and he was made captain. In fact, Graeme Souness called me in to explain that decision, probably because he realised I would be miffed after skippering Spurs and now being passed over when Butcher was out. Graeme told me that Robbo had been playing well but if he did not make him captain then he would be so upset that he would not perform for the team as he had been doing. 'I'll lose him completely', I can remember Graeme saying to me. The decision was made and there was not a great deal I could do about it but from then on we didn't have a good time. That's no reflection on Robbo's captaincy. It was just that we had injury problems and the enforced changes gave us a stuttering kind of season which brought no successes at all after the Skol Cup win.

It remains the worst season we have had at Ibrox since I joined the club. We lost to Dunfermline in the Scottish Cup – a disastrous result. And we dropped into third place in the Premier League behind Celtic, who were champions and Cup-winners in their centenary season, and Hearts who were in second place. And we went out of the European Cup to the Romanian team Steaua of Bucharest. I can still recall losing five games out of 11 in a dreadful sequence of results fo us. We missed Terry then but, also, things were not exactly right between Robbo and myself.

At half time in the second leg of the European Cup quarter-final we lost an early goal at Ibrox and we fell out. Badly! It was something we had talked about after the 2-0 defeat at their ground and it was something we knew we had to avoid at all costs if we were to give ourselves any chance of going through to the last four. Anyhow, their man ran between Robbo and me and scored. I thought he should have gone. He thought I should have gone and we had a bust-up at the interval. This was not the first time. We had had three rows before that one, all over more or less the same kind of thing. The partnership was not one which has been made in heaven. The Steaua row was a bad one though and it left me unhappy and unsettled in my relationship with Robbo.

It wasn't just our own problems which were upsetting me. I didn't think his treatment of the young players was right. He would give them stick and he would do it in a nasty kind of way. I didn't like it. I just did not approve of the way he talked to the younger players – nor the way he picked on others rather than accept blame himself when he got it wrong.

By now there was a lot of bickering among the players – the way things go when a team is doing badly. To some extent it was all falling apart in the dressing-room at that time.

It was not a happy time at the club. Graeme had always encouraged open discussion in the dressing-room. He favoured players having their say but there were a lot of strong personalities around then and too many people wanted their say in what was going wrong. Forwards were blaming the defence, we were having at go at the midfield and it was all getting totally out of hand. After the Steaua game there were a few heated discussions and the whole atmosphere was not helped by the fact that we had dropped so far behind Celtic in the title race. By the time we came to the last home game of the season we were out of it – but that still didn't help the manager's mood when we lost 1-0 to Aberdeen at Ibrox. It was almost as if this was the last straw and the much talked about confrontation between Graeme Souness and Robbo took place in the dressing-room after the match. We had lost a bad goal and we knew it. A ball had been played in and was cleared and as it went out of the box we all followed it except for Robbo. He stayed in there and when the ball was returned he was playing an Aberdeen attacker onside and they scored. He wouldn't accept the blame when we started our inquest at the end of the game. In the middle of this barney – and it was a barney – the manager arrived and he cut through it all by telling Robbo, 'It was your fault. I blame you.' And then when Robbo still wouldn't accept it he had a real go at him. He really tore into him. He told him that he was a Tottenham player who had got lucky and won a couple of medals and that was his whack. Robbo replied after Graeme's tirade had ended, 'If that's how you feel about it then why don't you just sell me?' And Graeme, sweet as you like, told him: 'When you are going out through that door just take your boots with you, son, and don't bother coming back.'

That was the end of Robbo's Rangers career. I heard all the stories of punches being thrown and all the rest but that didn't happen. Graeme was quite cold and calculated when he told him to take his boots.

There might just have been a way back for him if he had been content to keep a low profile . . . but that was not Robbo's way. He eventually over-estimated his value to the club because he believed that 'punter power' would save him. He was wrong.

Robbo had become a bit of a cult figure to the supporters and he clearly thought his popularity with them would bring a last-gasp reprieve. We had one more game to go. It was at Brockville against Falkirk and by now Robbo had been axed from the team and everyone knew of the dressing-room row. The news had swept through Glasgow and, inevitably with Rangers being Rangers, it had been front-paged in the newspapers.

For his own reasons Robbo came to Falkirk for that match and took his seat in the stand among the fans. He was cheered as he arrived and there were banners around the ground saying that Robbo must stay. He should have known better. It would not have mattered if every single Rangers' fan there that day had waved a banner in his support, the fact that he had embarrassed the club in public meant that he was finished. It was not a pleasant atmosphere in the stand that day for David Holmes, the club chairman, and it wasn't the best of days for Graeme Souness either. Both men were furious at the way the club's dirty linen was being washed in public. OK, people knew there had been trouble – but now Robbo was flaunting himself in front of the fans and encouraging them to support him against Graeme. There was only ever going to be one winner in that contest . . .

Before the start of the next season Robbo apparently tried to apologise to the manager for what had happened. But it had gone well beyond apologies making things right. Robbo was sent off with the third team to play pre-season games. He didn't train with the first-team squad and soon he was off to Chelsea. It was a move which had gone wrong – and I don't blame Graeme Souness in the slightest for what happened. Robbo tried to take him on. He tried it in the dressing-room in front of the players. Then he made his biggest mistake of all by trying to take him on in full public view at Brockville on that last Saturday of the season. It was his worst miscalculation. Graeme Souness ran the club at that time. He had transformed things at Ibrox. And he was not about to have that ruined by one player who was bearing a grudge.

Personally, I think Graeme saw something in Robbo's character which he didn't like. Perhaps he had felt that during the bad times we had had, Robbo was not a player you could rely on totally when the chips were down. There was a lot of disharmony in the dressing-room around that time and maybe Robbo had to go so that we could achieve the camaraderie that now exists at the club.

I had a couple of rucks with Chris Woods around that time, too. After one Dundee United game when we had lost a goal he was going to hang one on my chin. Then after we lost 2-1 to Celtic, which gave them the title, there was more bother between us. But there was no lasting aggravation the way there was with Robbo. Woodsy and I got together after that Celtic game, cleared the air and agreed that a few cobwebs had been swept away by our 'full and frank' discussion in the dressing-room! I was glad of that because Woodsy was a big lump of a lad and a punch on the jaw from him would have been severe.

In football, especially with big clubs who are playing for the major honours in the game, you are always liable to get flare ups. But since Robbo left after that row with Graeme Souness I can't recall too many serious ones. There have been a couple at training – the usual handbags at 20 paces but nothing too serious. And nothing lasting.

Then, of course, since then there have been five titles in succession, a Skol Cup or three and two Scottish Cup wins . . .

It's when you are on a losing run and pressure is building on you that you get trouble in the dressing-room. Often, too, you can pinpoint where the trouble will come from before it actually happens. I reckon I can sense impending trouble now and I know Walter will be able to do the same – probably quicker than I can. Fortunately no one has rocked the boat at all since Robbo's time and the team spirit has been good.

The other controversial arrival and departure was, of course, Mo Johnston. I had known Mo from our days together in the Scotland Under-21 team and he was a happy-go-lucky character then just as he was when he came to Rangers despite all the fuss and fury which surrounded the transfer.

Mo, in fact, was one of the few players who could have crossed that particular great divide without allowing it to upset him in the slightest. It wasn't just that he, as an ex-Celtic player, had agreed to sign for Rangers. Nor was it that he was the first high-profile Roman Catholic signing at the club. Mo, being Mo, had to have further complications surrounding the deal. His old club, Celtic, had moved in for him first when his spell with Nantes in France was coming to an end. He had signing talks with them at Parkhead and posed there for pictures with a Celtic jersey. Then there was, apparently, some kind of hitch. Graeme Souness stepped in, signed him and Celtic were left looking more than a little bit foolish.

Mo was the centre of attraction. He was the most talked about footballer in the country and that was just the way he liked it. The media fuss was enormous but there was not too much concern about it all in the dressing-room. Among the players there was just the feeling that the manager had signed a world-class striker – and that was to be welcomed!

As far as I was concerned Mo was playing the best football of his career when he joined us. Playing in France with Nantes had suited him. He was playing fewer games, he was looking after himself and was fantastically sharp. We had all seen that for ourselves when he had been back home for Scotland games. The religious aspects didn't worry the players any. We joked about that. When he came to our pre-season training camp in Italy at Il Ciocco he walked into the dining-room and found a table all on its own, off in a corner, and was told that was for him. He enjoyed that joke as much as anyone and I think it helped lighten things for him.

It was not an easy thing for him to do. He knew he was going to face opposition from both sets of supporters – every single Celtic fan would be against him because he had snubbed the club's signing offer. And, at the same time, some of our more diehard fans were not ready to accept him. He received threats and they were taken seriously enough by the club that they employed a 'minder' to look out for him. Mo arrived every day for training with this big guy tagging along and for a long time that was the way he lived his life off-field. Not too many players would have been able to cope with the situation. Mo did and was still able to retain his sense of humour.

He also retained his form. He was at peak fitness then and he was a great addition to the squad. He led the line superbly, linked up with other players intelligently and scored regularly. Who could have asked for anything more?

Mo was not particularly religiously minded so that brought few problems. Most of us had known him in the Scotland team and so he already had friends in the squad. And when he scored his first goal and kept on scoring – even against Celtic – he was accepted by the majority of the support. He took a little time to settle – after all the publicity it was a wonder that he was able to settle at all. And when he did he struck a rich seam of form.

In that first season with us he was unbelievable. In fact, for ten months or so, in spite of the off-field pressures he had to contend with every single day of his life, he was the perfect striker. He was working hard on the training ground, he was playing with verve and confidence and he was scoring freely.

Then in his second season I detected signs of the old Mo, the Mo we had known before that spell in France had given him a fresh lease of life. He was back in Scotland, things had quietened down after the initial furore and he

138

had his pals around him again. It was not a recipe for success. He began to go off the boil a bit. He was not as quick and he was having his two or three nights out a week with his mates. He would tell you himself that he was fond of a few nights out and they began catching up with him. He was OK to start with because Graeme Souness was still there and Graeme had signed him, but when Graeme left he was no longer first choice for the first team. He was sitting on the bench where Ally McCoist had had to sit so long and so patiently in the previous two seasons. The only thing was that Mo could not handle that the way Coisty did. He didn't want to be third choice behind Mark and Coisty and he put up his hand and said it would be better if he left and Walter agreed to let him go. Everton offered £1.2 million for him and he was sold to Goodison Park.

It had been a memorable time and an important one for the club. Mo Johnston's signing silenced the critics who slammed Rangers for pursuing sectarian policies. It was a brave decision by Graeme to sign him – and an even braver decision by Mo to come. The club owe him a debt for that as well as for the goals he scored.

CHAPTER TEN

Your Body is Your Bank

I suppose you could always have called me a fitness fanatic because I was brought up by my Dad to keep myself in condition. Now, though, allied to that, I have started to pay more attention to my diet. The influence of players who have been abroad, particularly those who were in Italy, has had a lot to do with that. I can still remember Ray Wilkins when he was at Ibrox telling me: 'Your body is your bank. That's what wins you medals. That's what gets you new contracts. That's what makes you money.' He warned me that once a player's fitness goes then he is finished. His advice was to take care of your body, always maintain the highest standards of fitness because once you drop those levels then clubs won't want you. Basically if you let yourself go, then the party's over.

I listened to him because, for me, he was a great professional. Still is in fact. He is 36 years old and he was still playing until last season's injury. He remained in marvellous condition because he looked after himself. He told me that when he was at Ibrox he was actually lighter than he had been at any other stage of his career. He had found that his best playing weight was less than it had been when he was a younger player.

As I said earlier, my Dad was always very fit. He had been a paratrooper and then he was a professional footballer. He used to take me out on training runs with him. I'd be about ten or 11 years old and he was playing in the Second Division out there in South Africa but still keeping himself in trim. So he would get me out of bed at six o'clock in the morning and I would go off running with him. We would finish off with some exercises and ever since then staying 100 per cent fit has been a part of my life.

I formed a close relationship with my Dad then which still exists to this day and the disciplines he taught me as a youngster have stood me in good stead ever since. His army background provided a strictness in my upbringing and he taught me to enjoy training. He was a strong man, and a fit man and a very disciplined man and even today he remains a very fit person. That's something I would like to follow. When I stop playing I'd like to think that I would keep up some kind of training regime. I'm sure that I will because I'd probably miss all the various disciplines if I was to neglect them. I've been training for so long now I'm sure that I would just continue at some level.

Training and working hard to keep yourself in the best physical shape possible has been with me all through those years. Watching what I eat and trying to have a balanced diet has only been a part of my preparations for a few years now. It was not something which I bothered about when I was a Dundee United player for instance. I was a youngster then and no one talked about diet in those days. Then, when I started to go with Scotland I used to watch what the other players ate and try to pick up some pointers as to how they looked after themselves. Obviously I'd look at the more experienced players because that's who you can learn from. So I studied Kenny Dalglish and Graeme Souness and while Kenny didn't bother too much about what he ate I noted a big change in Graeme once he moved to Italy.

It was obvious that the clubs there paid much more attention to what their players were eating. Graeme had picked up on that very quickly and he came home to join Scotland and tried to follow what he was being told to do at Sampdoria. Before his transfer he would eat the same as everyone else – afterwards it was different. He would ask for some pasta, or sometimes he would ask for some liver – just little changes he had picked up – and from about 1986 or so I began to do the same. I believe it's a natural progression for any player. When you are younger you can eat and drink more or less anything you want. When you get older then you know you have to take more care. Some players pay more attention than others do. In other countries, though, players seem to do it all through their careers and they go into it much more thoroughly than we ever do here in Britain.

I have definitely taken it all much more seriously the older I have become. I think the normal way of things is that a player gets to 30 or 31, decides he might be putting on weight and makes up his mind to cut down on the pints and the fish suppers. You really have to be a bit more careful than that.

Personally I have been lucky in the way I'm shaped and I have never had a weight problem at all. But over the past six or seven years I have taken increasing notice of what I eat and drink. I don't have any kind of elaborate plan. No daily or weekly or even monthly diet which I follow. There are just certain rules which I try to follow as closely as possible.

I stay clear of fats and I eat pasta a lot. Basically I watch what I am eating, trying to think what is best for me as an athlete. Some people cut out red meat completely – but I have never thought about that. I'm a big red meat fan. Growing up in South Africa where we used to have all these barbecues sorted out my taste buds early and there is no way I would change that. All I do now is trim the meat to take away any fat that might be on it. I find that good enough for me. I tend to view diet and training together and I feel that if I'm training regularly and training properly then it should not matter too much that I'm going to eat some red meat. As long as I'm avoiding the fat and not over-eating then I don't see a problem.

The pasta I eat – and I do eat it often – is a habit I picked up from the lads who were in Italy. It has become a staple of my diet and I feel it has been good for me. You have only to look at the players who spent time in Italian football to realise that introducing pasta to your diet works wonders. We had *four* at Ibrox – Graeme Souness, Trevor Francis, Ray Wilkins and Mark Hateley. All of them were able to play into their middle or late thirties and when you see Mark in action now you can recognise how superbly fit he is. They have all learned how to look after themselves and that's what I have tried to do as well. Injuries can shorten anyone's career and there is not a great deal you can do about them. But you do have control over your fitness and you can keep your level of fitness high. It is something which pays off for you in the long run. For instance, my weight has remained an almost constant 12 stone since I was a young player with Dundee United. If it does change then I do something about it. Fortunately, though, it stays more or less the same. You could call it my fighting weight.

Some people have suggested to me that that's a bit light for my height which is around six feet one or six feet two. And I remember Graeme Souness warning me that as you get older your body thickens and that you do need some extra bulk. But any time I have strayed a few pounds over

144

the twelve stone mark I have not felt sharp. I've felt a little sluggish, a little uncomfortable and so I keep a careful check on how much I weigh. That's something I have done all through my career, just tried to keep my weight as stable as possible. I'm pretty happy that I have been able to do that from being a teenager at Tannadice to being a near veteran with Rangers. As well as making me feel good physically it is a psychological boost to me, especially as I get older!

You know, even in the close season I keep an eye on the scales. I may have a binge or two like anyone else – but they are only occasional lapses from the disciplines I lay down for myself and if I put on a few pounds then I just get on the training gear and work off the extra. I want to play on for a few seasons yet and looking after my fitness is one way to guarantee that.

Basically I have one main meal a day. I have cereal and fruit juice in the morning, possibly a sandwich or something light at lunchtime and then a meal at night. On match days I have a little cereal at 11 o'clock when it's an afternoon game, and when we play an evening match I have some pasta at lunchtime and that's it.

I don't drink as much now as I used to either. As a young player I used to go out with the rest of the lads and have a few pints of beer but over the years I have toned that down a lot mainly because I realised that to be as professional as possible then you should be cautious about drinking.

I enjoy a glass of lager and I drink South African beers when I'm at home – not that I'm much of a house drinker. I may take some wine with a meal or a glass of champagne when I'm out for dinner. But I don't really bother too much any more. When I was young it didn't bother me but as you get older you like to think you also get a little wiser. You definitely grow to appreciate that it is your fitness which earns you a good living and you take extra precautions so as not to put that at risk. That's what I have tried to do. Again, to be honest, when I was a young player I could go out with the lads and have a few drinks and the next day at training I'd be fine. Now, on the odd occasion I have a night out I find training the next morning is hard work. That's just a reality you have to accept.

I also happen to believe that when you are being paid well by a club for your services then you have a professional obligation to keep yourself in the best possible shape. When you are with a club as big as Rangers then it becomes even more important that any player keeps himself in the very top condition physically. A club such as Rangers looks after you – it is then your duty to keep yourself right for them. After all they are not paying you good money to have you sitting around in a boozer all afternoon when you finish training. Or to be hanging around clubs at night when you have training the following day. If you behave that way then you are letting down the club and you are also letting down yourself and your profession. I am not suggesting for one minute that players should not have a drink or that they should live like monks. I've already said that there are times when I have a few. But there is a time and a place for everything and there is a responsibility attached to being a Rangers player. In my own case there is also an extra responsibility because I am the club captain. I take that seriously.

Over the last few years I have not gone out a great deal because there are always times in Glasgow when you can find trouble waiting for you and more often than not it comes when you are least expecting it. So I quite consciously took a little step back and I just don't go out and about all that very much now. I just don't think it's worth all the potential hassle.

Also, when I did go out the stories that did the rounds were ridiculous. If you went into any place in the city and had a few beers then by the time the reports filtered back to Ibrox you had been legless. I reckoned I didn't need any of that kind of aggravation. So I worked out a discipline which suits my lifestyle and my job as captain of Rangers. Sacrificing a few nights out is not a high price to pay for the career I enjoy at Ibrox. I consider that I have reached the very top of my profession and anyone who reaches that level in any walk of life has to give up certain things. I simply say to myself that when I'm 35 or 36 or whenever the time comes for me to stop playing, then I'll have plenty of time to do the things I have cut out of my life now.

If I want to sit in a pub all day then I can do that. If I want to spend every night of the week at clubs then I can do that too.

But, right now, that is not the road to go down and I can quite happily live without the pubs and the clubs. There is plenty of time for that when I stop playing *if* I want to spend my time that way. Mind you, I don't see myself every doing it because I'm not particularly that type of person.

Right now being captain at Ibrox is very, very important to me. I see it as an honour I have to try to live up to. There have been so many great captains at this club down through the years and most of them, like myself, captained Scotland too.

There is a tradition which surrounds the club and which surrounds the captaincy. I may not show it – I'm not a very demonstrative person – but all of this means a great deal to me. It has become a very important part of my life. I don't go to a lot of supporters' club functions and I don't go on to the pitch waving to the fans because that's not my way of going about things. I am a private person and I guard my privacy away from the game. But that does not diminish my respect for the captaincy or for the club, nor does it lessen my affection for the fans.

I would never do anything which would embarrass Rangers Football Club. In fact I would never do anything which might hurt the club or damage its reputation. All I want is that Rangers fans – and anyone else for that matter – can look back at my time here and see that I was a good ambassador for Rangers. I hope they will be able to do that and that they will also be able to say that I was a successful captain.

Only three others skippered the team to 'trebles' – Jock Shaw, Bobby Shearer and John Greig – so I have earned one little niche in the club's history.

I just hope that people can understand that I am a private person who tries to live a life outside the glare of publicity which surrounds Rangers in Glasgow. Just because I don't give public demonstrations of how I feel doesn't mean I care less than others. I care about Rangers as much as any of the supporters do. All I want is to help bring the club success and, perhaps, join the list of captains who are remembered by the support and celebrated by them long after their years of playing are over.

CHAPTER ELEVEN

Troubled Giants

I spent just over a year with Spurs after moving from Dundee United and football-wise it was a happy time for me. The manager then, David Pleat, and his Chairman, Irving Scholar, were both football men and they put together an incredibly talented team.

We had Ray Clemence in goal, of course, and then there were Danny Thomas and Mitchell Thomas at full-back and in midfield we had Ossie Ardilles and Glen Hoddle and Chrissy Waddle. My partner at the centre of the defence was Gary Mabbutt – who is still a mate of mine – and all we had to do was win the ball, give it forward to the midfield and then watch in admiration at their skills.

It was a tremendous side and we were very unlucky not to take at least one honour in that season. We lost to Arsenal in the League Cup, in the third game of a semi-final clash; came close to the First Division title for a spell during the season, and then lost in the Cup final to Coventry. That was a major disappointment for me. By then David Pleat had made me club skipper and it would have been marvellous to hold that trophy aloft at Wembley.

I never had another chance of a medal down there

because during the summer I had personal problems starting to surface which eventually I found too difficult to handle. My wife Lesley was homesick and she wanted to go back to Scotland to be closer to her mother in Dundee. She also wanted to take my son Michael back north of the border with her.

By now I had signed a fresh contract with Spurs – a five-year deal which the Chairman had offered to me because he was so happy with how my first season had gone. Gary Mabbutt signed one at the same time and it looked as if our partnership was to be important to the White Hart Lane club as they chased the major honours in English football. I thought that too – then my wife went back north and I had to face up to a crisis off the field. I didn't want to be separated from Michael as he was growing up.

Spurs were very understanding. At one point the Chairman suggested that the club would pay my fare home after a game on a Saturday to allow me to spend time with the family and then bring me back down to London. But I knew that would never work properly. It was a tremendous gesture by Irving Scholar but I could not see myself doing justice to the job I had with Spurs if I was flying back and forth to Scotland all the time.

They wanted me as club captain and it would have been impossible to continue as skipper and play consistently year after year when my home life was so disrupted. Reluctantly I told them that I had to be transferred back to Scotland. Equally reluctantly they finally agreed to sell me. It was not an easy decision for me. I had been happy there. The future at that time looked bright. But if you are unhappy you cannot give your best on the field and fortunately David Pleat and Irving Scholar recognised that in their talks with me. I still have great admiration for both men and I know I owe them a debt of gratitude for being so understanding at that difficult period of my career.

Rangers moved in when they heard that I was so unsettled – and, to be honest, that's where my heart was. No other club had a chance when I knew Graeme Souness wanted me, though before any deal could be finalised I had the chance to stay in England but move closer to home.

The success I expected for Spurs never really materialised and that has been a matter of some sadness for me because I will always look on them as one of the top clubs in the country. That is the status their tradition has earned them and now, with Ossie Ardilles back, I'm sure their great days will arrive.

I became close to Ossie in my time there. We lived close to each other and I used to go round to his home to speak about the game with him. I like to think that I picked up a lot from him because I found him very knowledgeable. He is a very intelligent man – you could always see that in his play. He used to do things in games and you would think to yourself that he had thought it all out beforehand. As well as that natural talent he had it was interesting for me to get a football viewpoint from a foreign player. Here was someone from another powerful soccer nation and I had the chance to hear about his approach to the game. You can pick up little bits here and there when you are playing teams from abroad – but this was a unique chance to play with an international player, at his peak a world-class player, from another country and then talk to him for hour after hour about the game.

He has had success as a manager and I know he had a deep feeling for Spurs as a club – if anyone can restore the great days and bring honours back to White Hart Lane then he is that man. I have kept in touch with him on a regular basis since I left London and I believe that he can do the job the fans want.

I don't know what went on at the club after I left, but I was upset when David Pleat left and just as upset when Irving Scholar departed. There have been numerous boardroom rows and no club ever prospers with that kind of background. If Ossie's arrival can heal the rift between the club and some of the fans then watch Spurs go.

There are some parallels which can be drawn between Spurs and our great Glasgow rivals Celtic in that area. There have been problems at Parkhead too, and in the last four years Celtic have not been able to win a trophy. For some of the time they have not even been our closest rivals – last year Aberdeen challenged harder than they did for example. And while some of the Rangers fans may revel in this I don't join them. I believe that Scottish football needs a strong Rangers and a strong Celtic too. I find it worrying that Celtic have not been as strong as they once were. I reckon that we need Celtic to be stronger. For them to be without a trophy in four long years is not something I take satisfaction in. Don't get me wrong: I want to help Rangers to new records. I want to captain them to their sixth title in a row, which would be a new record for the club. I would like to see them go on and beat Celtic's nine-in-a-row sequence. But I recognise the need for the age-old rivalry between the two clubs to continue. Rangers went a long time without a title win during the glory years when Jock Stein was in charge at Celtic. More recently the club went a long time without a Scottish Cup win. But there were other trophies and the gap between the two clubs did not seem to be as great.

They don't seem to have the money available to go out and buy top quality international players the way Rangers do. They don't seem to have the financial resources off the field that we do. And while I make no judgment, their boardroom affairs – it is no concern of mine after all – seem to have been problematical. All of these things would weaken any club's challenge.

Scotland is not big enough to lose the powerful presence of a top-rate Celtic. I played in London 'derby' games between Spurs and Arsenal – they were big occasions but none of them had the passion of an Old Firm clash. These games are unique and they have to remain meaningful. If one side becomes far stronger than the other then even the 'derbies' would become less important. That would be a tragedy for the clubs and for Scottish football.

We need the rivalry and while it brings its problems I have to say I have rarely suffered because of that in Glasgow. If I'm out and Celtic fans speak to me I have always found them to be OK. Some have even gone as far as saying they wished I was playing for them. That is never likely to happen but it's nice to think you can win that kind of respect from the opposition fans. Sure, they'll boo me at Parkhead but that doesn't hurt any and I like to think that my relationship with them over the years has been good.

I want to beat them every time we play. They want to see us lose. That's OK. It's natural. But if the gap grows any wider between the clubs then the rivalry might become more parochial than important. I don't want to see that happen. All over the world people talk about the Old Firm games. Let's keep it that way . . . with Rangers on top but not outrunning Celtic on every front.

This game of ours thrives on rivalry. But it has to be close rivalry. And I don't mind how close it gets as long as Rangers can still come out on top as best team in the country. We have a few more records in our sights after last season's treble and we aim to achieve all of them. What I'm saying is that I would like to see Celtic get stronger again – but not too strong!